FLOWER ARRANGING

Flowers can be used for every occasion—to enhance your furnishings, decorate your table and inspire your party. They can become the conversation piece at a social function, breaking the ice between awkward guests, or they can be the object of much attention in a competition. Advice on each is contained in this book. Whichever way you like flowers, simplicity should be the keynote to good flower arranging. Everything is told here from when to pick flowers and how to transport them, to drying them and creating them into actual arrangements. Oriental arrangements are dealt with, too. Color harmony is important, and it is essential for a beginner to understand this. The color wheel and chart will serve as explanation.

Different flowers require different types of arrangements and different containers. It is surprising just how many varied objects can be employed when one searches for holders. Most plant material arranges well, fruit, leaves, vegetables and seed heads—even wood can be used effectively.

Hopefully, with this book as a guide, even beginners can find a worthwhile hobby that is bound to bring them hours of enjoyment, and plenty of praise.

A
GROSSET
ALL-COLOR GUIDE

FLOWER ARRANGING

BY VIOLET STEVENSON

Illustrated by George Thompson, June Baker
and Elsie Wrigley

GROSSET & DUNLAP
A NATIONAL GENERAL COMPANY
Publishers • New York

Published Simultaneously in Canada

Library of Congress Catalog Card No.: 76-120434
Printed in the United States of America

CONTENTS

INTRODUCTION

Quite the best way of teaching is by example and, in the past, I have been fortunate in having been given the opportunity to show my kind of flower arranging, and so, through the medium of both words and pictures, to pass on my experience to others. However, this is the first time I have been given the opportunity to teach in a book which is completely in color. What a wonderful advantage this is! One can write forever about color harmonies, contrasts and analogies; one can try to explain the subtleties of tinge and shade of tone and hue, but words are not enough. How much better to be able to say what I mean by showing my flower arrangements entirely in color.

If flowers are to be arranged both attractively and skillfully it follows that one must know and understand what lies behind the skill of the art of flower arrangement. There are certain rules which can be followed, although perhaps these are better described as guide lines rather than rigid laws. There are also many tricks of the trade which can be used to save time and materials. Some can be used to make cut

Flower arrangement means value for money. By placing a few blooms in a simple pattern you display each one to its full advantage.

Even in large, glorious decorations each flower should have room to breathe. Simple, easy to follow rules, aid the arranger.

flowers last as long as possible; others help us to preserve and keep them and so to enable us to enjoy their beauty for a little longer.

A firm maxim of mine is that besides being esthetically beneficial, flower arrangement is also absolutely practical, for it is value for money! If you understand this maxim you can display as little as one flower and make a decoration of it. And yet, should your garden be full of bloom, you can fill your house with flowers in the shortest possible time in such a way that they will enhance their surroundings and reward you with a wonderful sense of achievement.

GOOD BEGINNINGS

If you want your flowers to live for many days after you have brought them home from the shop, you must see that they are in the best condition when you buy them. When I see lovely flowers on sale, I am always reminded of a market wholesaler who told me that a grower had just telephoned him to say that he had a greenhouse full of flowers which at that moment were looking as beautiful as he, the grower, had ever seen them. 'If that's the case, you keep them!' my friend told him. 'They are no good to me if they look absolutely beautiful to you! I want them looking that way after they reach the customers!'

Many flowers ought to be sold only in bud: all narcissi, including daffodils, iris, tulips, most lilies and many other bulb flowers, all of which will mature in water. Not only will these flowers travel better in bud and become less damaged, but they will live longer indoors and you will have the extra pleasure of watching them open into full-grown blooms and change daily before your eyes.

A flower's true function is either to pollinate another or to become pollinated itself, or maybe both. Once this happens and the flower reaches maturity it will begin to fade and nothing can prevent it. Some flowers take longer to reach

this point but obviously, the younger a flower is, the longer it will last. Ripe and/or spilled pollen is an indication that a flower has already reached or even passed maturity.

Double- and full-petalled flowers, like chrysanthemums, that show no central cluster of stamens, should show instead a central zone of young petals, still tight enough to make a dimple in the flower's center. If you see a curled, thread-like anther rising above the petals of a double flower, such as a carnation, it is likely to be much too old for you to buy, and you should avoid doing so. The stem ends should look wholesome, with no signs of slime, decomposing foliage or brown stains.

(*Left*) All narcissi should be bought in bud. Supplement week-old blooms with new buds, either together in a vase or apart, as they are in this little brass balance. (*Right*) Young chrysanthemums have a central dimple of young, often green petals. Anemones have immature sepals and no spilled pollen on the base of the petals. Gladiolis should have only the lower floret opening. Narcissi should be in bud. Tulip petals should still be curled under.

All types of poppies should be cut just as they are breaking from the bud. Crumpled petals will gradually expand and become smooth.

How and when to gather flowers

If you go into the garden early to gather flowers, you are more likely to catch them just as they are breaking bud and before the bees have visited and pollinated them. After a long cool night, stems should be swollen and cells well filled with water.

Roses are said to last longest in sunny weather if they are cut at midday. If roses are picked when too tight in bud, the petals will never expand properly. The calyx of sepals, which covers the petals and protects them when young, should be growing outward and downward. It is safest to wait until at least one of the petals has begun to grow away from the mass.

Many of the daisy family will not take water well after cutting unless the flowers are at the right stage. The ray florets should have expanded fully, although the disc florets, those which form the center 'eye', should still be immature.

Almost all bulb flowers can be picked in bud when the color of the bloom is beginning to show. However, if you want the bulb to produce flowers the following year, either cut the

Where flowers grow several to a stem, wait until the first bloom is open and then cut. Then the younger flowers and buds will mature as the first one fades. Be sure to cut sweet peas with sharp scissors. Do not try to pull them from the vine.

Rose buds can be cut too early in which case they will never open nicely in water. No matter what type, modern or old-fashioned, double or single, the calyx gives one a guide. Wait until the sepals begin to grow outward and downward.

leafy stem as short as possible, or in the leafless flower stalks, like narcissi, try to cut as few leaves as possible. Take one or two only from each plant. When narcissi buds crook to the 'gooseneck' stage, they are perfect for cutting.

Gladiolus and other flowers which have a similar mode of growth should be showing color just in the lowest floret.

Lilies should be just breaking bud. Reflexed petals should not yet have begun to turn back. Some people remove the pollen bearing anthers as soon as the petals open. Rhododendrons may be cut as soon as the buds are sticky. Blossom and early flowering shrubs may be cut after the turn of the year on a moist but not freezing day.

To help stems take water quickly, split the ends upward for an inch.

How to harden flowers

If flowers are to keep their first fresh appeal they must not be allowed to wilt. All flowers and foliage should be 'hardened' before being used in an arrangement by being given a long, deep drink. Sometimes they will wilt inexplicably after having been arranged. One way to avoid this is to always use tepid water, not only for the first drink but also at the time of arrangement.

(*Left*) Cutting stems above the thick nodes. (*Below*) Removing alternate leaves from stocks. (*Right*) Covering hellebores cutting stem ends under water and stripping stem ends.

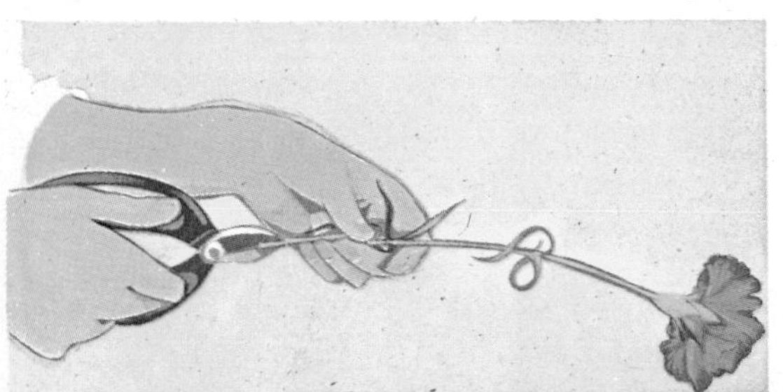

In simplest terms, a flower uses the same pores to give off moisture as it does to breathe. If, because of adverse conditions, it gives off more water than can be replaced, the flower wilts. While any cut flower is out of water it still breathes but it is also losing essential moisture. It is not enough merely to stand the stem end in water, but if the stems and leaves can be covered no water can be lost and the stem cells will quickly conduct water to the flower.

This is why it is good to give most flowers and leaves a long, deep drink before arrangement. The few exceptions to this rule are dealt with later. However, before the stems are placed in water they need attention to ensure that they can function properly. One of the main causes of wilting is air bubbles which form in the stem when the flower is cut, thus preventing the flow of water from the stem end to the bloom. All that is usually necessary to remedy this is to recut the stem a little higher up before replacing it immediately in water.

Another method, good for hollow stems such as delphiniums, is to recut the stem under water. Both splitting the stem upward and cutting it on a long slant are effective for many types of flowers.

Where there are many leaves, and especially if the blooms have soft petals, it may be necessary to remove some to cut down the area from which moisture will be lost. Stocks and many other flowers last longer if every other leaf is carefully cut off. This retains the character of the flower which is lost if the stem is completely defoliated. Certainly all leaves on that part of the stem to go under water should be removed. Leaves very near a bloom, where they are likely to hide the flower, as with roses, should be cut away.

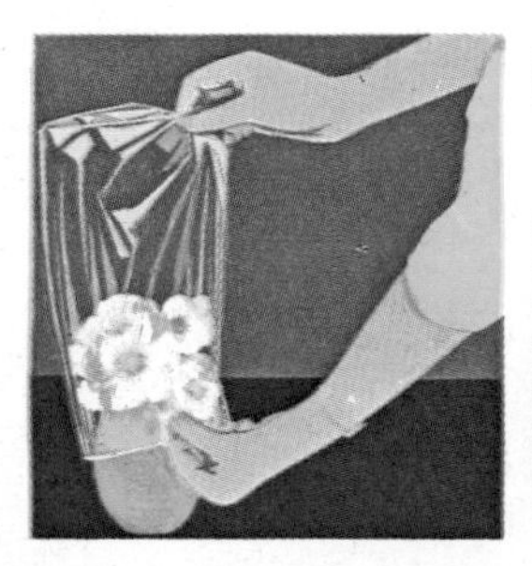

Delicate flowers like gypsophila, fern fronds, young tender leaves or anything else of great frailty should be gently drawn through water.

How to transport flowers

If they have not been properly wrapped, many flowers fade on the way home. Usually, standing their stems in tepid water after recutting the ends is sufficient to help them become turgid again but sometimes a little first-aid is needed. Water is heavy and if these flowers or leaves are immersed in it, even for a minute, they become bruised, damaged and

When you buy flowers in winter see that the florist envelops them entirely so that not only are the stem ends covered but also the blooms. In very cold weather a double layer of paper will keep out the cold.

discolored. Instead, frail flowers and foliage should be gently drawn through a bowl of water so that some of the moisture is held on the petals like dew.

After this, gently shake them so that the surplus water is swished off, recut the stem ends and stand them in tepid water to harden. Although this method is the salvation of some flowers, others spoil if allowed to remain wet; sweet peas and pansies are examples of these. Deterioration, however, can always be prevented by shaking flowers to dry them.

If flowers are to be transported, cut and pack them while they are dry. Do not give them a drink first. It is best to pack them in such a way that they lose little moisture. Remember that the best packing material for a flower is another flower. Those packed tightly in a box or plastic bag are less likely to come to as much harm as those in which moss or paper has been used to separate the flowers. If a box has to be lined with paper see that it is non-absorbent.

I find that the best way of all to transport flowers is to use strong, transparent plastic bags. They are best packed either according to their stem lengths or to their kind. Roses should not be packed with soft-petalled flowers in case the thorns damage them. Place the flowers upright, stem first, in the bag. There should be a good space between the top of the flowers and the opening of the bag, for this cushion of air will protect them. Sappy flowers such as nasturtiums and soft velvety ones like pansies are best packed in a shallow tin or plastic food box with a well-fitting lid. Keep both bags and boxes out of sunshine. If flowers are left too long in plastic bags, especially at high temperatures, they will turn black.

A strong plastic bag is one of the best containers for transporting flowers. If the stem ends of roses are dethorned before they are packed and plenty of foliage is left on the stems, the plastic is not as likely to be torn. The bag should be made as airtight as possible so that no moisture is lost on the journey.

Violets must have humid conditions or they quickly die. One way to keep them is in wet gravel in a brandy snifter or glass bowl.

Helping flowers to live longer

The most important factor in helping flowers to live longer is that both the containers and the water should be clean. Always wash vases after use. To keep the water clean and wholesome, see that the portion of stem which is to go under water is stripped of foliage. Most leaves begin to decompose once they are immersed, which speeds up bacterial activity in the water. The worse offenders are members of the daisy family. Rose leaves are not likely to begin to decay before the flowers fade and, in fact, it is advisable to let some of these remain on the stem, even if they are under water, because they are known to feed the blooms. Evergreens also take a long time to decompose. But, generally speaking, it is best to take the lower leaves off.

Flowers respond to some form of plant food in the water. A teaspoonful of sugar or honey added to a pint of water are helpful ingredients for keeping flowers alive for a longer period of time.

When branches of blossom or evergreens are expected to stand for many days, a little soluble plant food helps to sustain them. Rose nutrients and other preservatives can be bought.

If these foods are to be added it is doubly important that the water does not become fouled. It is a fact that aspirin helps to keep water clean but only because it helps to delay bacterial activity. A copper coin has much the same effect, and water keeps sweeter in metal containers but fouls quicker in glass. Some of the foamed plastic stem holders, such as Florapak, contain formaldehyde which acts as a deterrent to decay. A few small nuggets of charcoal help to keep water sweet. Rain water is better than tap water.

Some flowers such as sweet peas, live longest in shallow water. Almost all bulb flowers last best this way, but forced tulips should first be stood in deep water to harden. The leafless kinds really do not need hardening.

If a flower, other than a bulb one, has wilted very badly, stand the stem in two inches of boiling water.

Flowers last longer if they are given certain easily assimilated foods. Sugar and proprietary nutrients can be added to the water.

It is not necessary to change the flower water daily but in shallow containers, best for bulb flowers, water evaporates and should be replaced.

Blossom lasts longest if it is undisturbed. A container with a narrow aperture prevents evaporation. From time to time add a little soluble plant food. Water in a metal container keeps sweeter longer than in those of other materials.

Care and treatment of arranged flowers

Once flowers have been arranged it should not be necessary to disturb them again until the decoration is changed. If the water has become dirty, change it by taking the entire arrangement to the tap and let fresh water pour into some part of the container.

In hot rooms many flowers and leaves benefit by a light spray of clean room-temperature water. Flowers which grow in cool conditions, like violets, react favorably to this. Chrysanthemums live longer if petals and leaves are sprayed once or twice a day. Full-petalled blooms like carnations seem to be prevented from becoming 'sleepy' too quickly.

Sometimes flowers wilt inexplicably. To revive them, remove them from the arrangement, recut the stem ends and stand them in two inches of boiling water until the water cools. This method can be used on all flowers except those which grow from bulbs, because the boiling water will 'cook' the stems. If tulips wilt, recut the stems under water. If the stem end is much lighter than the rest cut all the pale portion away. Stand in deep, tepid water to harden.

Lilac and other shrubs, garden fresh or forced, sometimes wilt badly after cutting. Cut away all leafy side stems, split these stem ends also and arrange them separately.

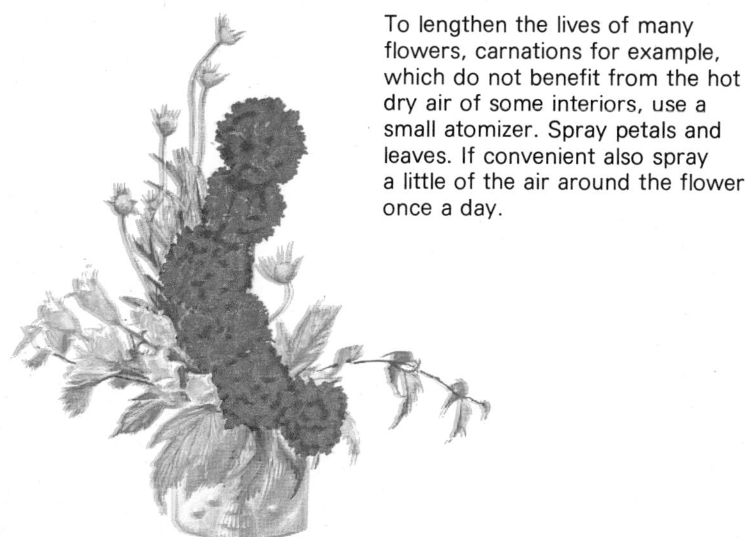

To lengthen the lives of many flowers, carnations for example, which do not benefit from the hot dry air of some interiors, use a small atomizer. Spray petals and leaves. If convenient also spray a little of the air around the flower once a day.

Every color of the spectrum can be found in flowers. Foliage, stems, seeds and fruits bring a variety of hues, tones, tints and shades.

THE IMPORTANCE OF COLOR

The colors of the rainbow are the ones to be found throughout nature. These are known as the spectrum. Among them are three primary colors: red, yellow and blue. The secondary colors, orange, green and purple, are derived from combinations of primary colors. In a rainbow the primary colors appear to overlap to produce the secondary colors and we can see that blue and yellow give green, and yellow and red give orange. If we make the spectrum into a star we can see how red and blue overlap to give purple.

In a rainbow there always appears to be the same degree of light. Sometimes we see it more clearly when the colors seem more intense and we can say that they have a good tone but we do not see a dark rainbow or a very pale one. However, the colors around us vary much more. Dark ones which appear to have black in them are called shades.

Light colors that appear to have white or light added to them are known as 'tints'. 'Hues' describe those which lie between the true spectrum colors. A forest may appear uniformly green, but when you look more carefully you will see that it is composed of may kinds, or hues, of green.

If the spectrum colors are arranged in a star we can see that certain colors are opposite each other. It happens that these have a natural affinity and are known as complementaries. Thus, blue is complementary to orange, red to green and yellow to purple. When these are mixed we find that they make familiar 'safe' colors. Blue and orange make a gray, red and green make a brown, and purple and yellow make a tan. All these are 'broken' colors.

Other colors may also be broken. It is worthwhile playing with a paint-box for an hour or two to discover what clear colors lie in any broken color, for these are found in many natural materials and are therefore useful.

If the rainbow colors are isolated and arranged in a star in their natural sequence, we can see that they have a natural affinity.

Color harmony

As you become more familiar with flowers you will learn much about color harmony from them, but in the meantime you can be guided by the color wheel. The neighboring colors, those which lie side by side, create natural analogous harmonies. Because we are dealing with flowers and not manufactured materials, these harmonies are the easiest to create.

We can create two-color analogous harmonies, but these are not always quite as satisfying or pretty as those in which three colors are used. Once again, because we are using flowers and not, say, fabrics, we are more likely to find that the three colors which we have chosen are of varying intensity.

Some colors are much more dominating than others. Red flowers in an arrangement tend to dominate the rest, but if this is not desirable one color can always be toned down by using a greater proportion of some other color to balance its stridency. You will find that broken colors are often helpful in this respect. And these broken colors should contain the true color, by which I mean that to balance red, use brown, which contains red mixed with green.

Many dried and preserved materials are in broken colors. Pleasant harmonies can be made by using them with one or more of the clear colors from which they are made. Here there are also tints of the brown made by mixing red and green.

Complementary harmonies, though natural, are sometimes a little strong for some tastes. Orange and blue flowers, for example, in a large decoration might dominate a room but the same harmony made from tints of the same colors, in this case soft apricot and pale blue, might prove more pleasing. It all depends on the interior of the room or the setting in which the flowers are to be placed. Fortunately, in flower decoration green is almost always present in the form of leaves or stems or other parts of the flower and this helps to form either a link or a buffer between one flower and another.

Color can deepen in intensity from a tint, which is the color with light or alternatively white added to it, to a shade which is the color with shadow or black added. We speak of the variations in color values as tones of a color.

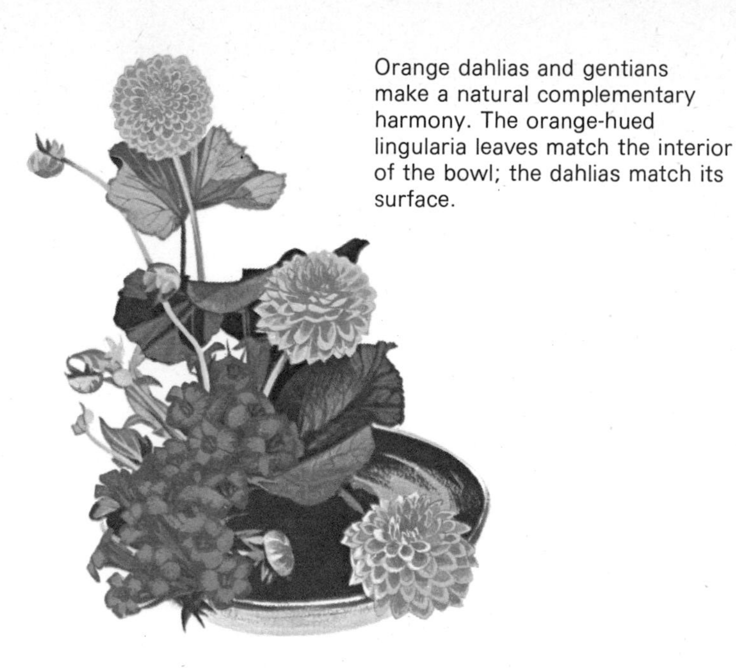

Orange dahlias and gentians make a natural complementary harmony. The orange-hued lingularia leaves match the interior of the bowl; the dahlias match its surface.

It is seldom possible to make color harmonies of flowers in the same way that we could make them from paints or lengths of cloth. Flowers contain within their petals, stems, foliage and other parts, many colors, not all of which are evident from a casual glance. This means that if we want a two-color harmony it is likely we shall find that other colors do creep in. A flower's stems, stamens, even leaves may be a bright green and although it is possible to defoliate a stem, it is not always desirable, for the sake of the flowers or even sometimes for their appearance. So we must compromise.

Quite often leaves colored other than green can be used either to emphasize the floral color or to hide the existing green foliage and stems. This is one reason why it is wise, if you have a garden, to grow a good stock of plants which will produce leaves as well as, or even instead of, flowers. Sometimes you will find that the under-surface of leaves may be more colorful than the upper.

Flowers often point the way to analogous harmonies by the way that types of flower may vary in color. Thus, you

A blue glass and purple sweet peas set the theme for this analogous harmony. Anchusa, columbines, geranium, delphiniums and anemones contribute toward it.

will find that nasturtiums, for instance, all have colors and hues that can be arranged together in harmony. This cannot be taken as an infallible rule because man has interfered with nature's color plan, and where once only two primary colors were ever present in a genus the hybridist has presented a third, often taking us out of the analogous zone. For example, once sweet peas could be said to follow through from the reds to the purples, but the hybridist is endeavoring to introduce yellow. However, in general, the above rule stands, and it is very helpful to the flower arranger who can take some flowers, say cornflowers, and arrange them together knowing that she is well on the way to creating a pleasant harmony. Her next step is to look for other flowers or plant materials that also carry the colors, perhaps in tints or shades, of the mixed cornflowers which she has chosen as the basis of her color scheme.

Often the container in which the flowers are to be arranged will supply a missing color. In analogous harmonies it is important that the container is considered part of the color scheme, so enhancing the design.

Sprays of blackberries in varying degrees of ripeness suggested the colors for this arrangement.

Learning about color

As I said earlier, no flowers have one pure color, and by studying a flower an arranger can learn more about floral color than by any other method. Quite often an idea for a lovely color harmony is found in the heart of a tulip. Perhaps the petals are pink, at their bases you can see a zone of deep blue, the anthers are creamy, the stems and foliage a soft jade green. Here is your color scheme ready for you to follow. Plan to use the colors in much the same proportion as you see them in the flower.

Take another lesson. Perhaps you do not want to use a particular flower, but it has just the color that you have in your furnishings. Take a flower that contains other colors at its center, on the underside of its petals, foliage, or even buds and thorns, and compare those colors not only with other self-colored blooms but also with containers.

Since flower arrangement has become so popular I have met many people who have told me how 'doing the flowers' has taught them to see with new eyes.

It is fascinating to find that floral colors are not always what they seem. Take pink for example, I imagine that most of us think that we know that pink is a tint of red, but once we begin comparing floral color we find, in fact, that the pink we know most, that is the pink of cherry blossom, of sweet peas, peonies and carnations, is in fact a tint of spectrum purple! Salmon pink is a tint of red.

Earlier I recommended that one experiment with colors to find what lay behind the broken colors, but it is also well worthwhile spending some time diluting water colors to discover more about their tints. After this, spend a little time adding black to a color so that you can make a mental color scale of colors you know well.

Autumn leaves offer thrilling lessons in color for their harmonies are gorgeous! If you want to make a special seasonal arrangement look for a multi-colored leaf to be your guide.

The brown centers of the annual chrysanthemums seemed to ask for this container. It is also the 'broken color' of the red and greens.

Monochromatic arrangements

If you have a piece of really dark glass which you would like to use as a container for your flowers, hold it up to the light and find its true color and then arrange matching flowers in it. If you select some flowers which have a tint of the color and others which have a full tone you will, in effect, have made a floral color scale on one color.

Your arrangement would be pleasing but it might not be obvious to everyone that you have taken just one color as your theme as it would if you placed white flowers in white.

Monochromatic arrangements can be both beautiful and dramatic. Perhaps more than any others they can set the mood of an interior or even of an occasion. In my country home I have white walls, and I find that there is an almost breathtaking beauty about a white arrangement against a white background. It is particularly tranquil. Yet for drama, the same arrangement seen against a contrasting background, would have the desired effect.

Some arrangers (I consider them over-zealous) become so obsessed with the idea of monochrome that they not only defoliate a stem to banish green if this is not required, but also remove parts of the flower should they be of another color. Frankly, I do not take flower arrangement color seriously enough ever to be likely to do this. Instead, even when I am planning monochromatic schemes, I accept the

All-green arrangements can be both lovely and enduring. Not only the leaves are green; there are also green flowers, fruits, seed heads, calyces and, in this case, candles.

fact that a little green is likely to creep through and that some of my flowers are likely to have centers which contrast with or differ from the main color. As a matter of fact, I like them best this way.

It seems to me inevitable that green is always with us and many would not prefer it otherwise. It never fails to fascinate me that while we all love flowers for their color's sake and, one would assume, for the fact that these colors offer a contrast to the ubiquitous green, green flowers have a tremendous appeal to arrangers and gardeners alike. Many of them are of great beauty.

I think that I am right in believing that there are more monochromatic arrangements made in green than in any other color and they are interesting to assemble and plan.

Monochromatic arrangements in which container and flowers match can be very beautiful as well as practical. This is a good way to display bought flowers.

Fruit and leaves can play their own role in monochromatic arrangements. Contrasting croton leaves extend the color of lemons and anemone-centered chrysanthemums in a long trough.

This arrangement was designed for my white-walled country bedroom. The colors of apple blossom, scillas and anemones and variegated kale match the patterned carpet.

Flowers as furnishings

If you grow your own flowers, plan to cultivate those which will suit your home. If you have to shop for your materials, buy those which will harmonize with your surroundings rather than those which happen to catch your eye.

Flower arrangements ought not to be dominant in your home. Instead they should fit into it like any other ornament you display. It is important that the container for the flowers should be well chosen. If your tast is for antique furniture then you may need to choose some vessel that will not detract from the beauty of the piece upon which it stands.

Not all homes can be classified by style so clearly. The flower decorations in most homes can be linked to the furnishings very simply, as I have already shown, by color. Sometimes a definite theme is most effective; for example, an arrangement could be staged below or near a painting, the colors of which can be repeated by the flowers.

If your soft furnishings are patterned you may do best to

choose one of the colors represented and to use this as the main theme in the flower arrangements with perhaps just the lightest touch here and there of the other colors. But, I fear that if you place mixed arrangements near patterned material, neither will be shown to advantage.

If you treat a flower arrangement as a piece of furniture you are more likely to achieve success. Perhaps there are not many flat surfaces on which flowers can be placed and if this is the case, consider using a pedestal in a corner to display your floral arrangements. There are many lovely torchères, once used to hold a candle or oil lamp, which can be used for this purpose. A wall vase or a wall bracket are means of displaying flowers without encroaching on floor or table space.

Use flowers to create illusions. Place vivid, dramatic arrangements at the end of a very long room. Conversely, arrange them on a wall opposite the door of a room which is too narrow. Use pastel tints and metal vessels to brighten dark interiors or to bring light to dark corners.

Metal containers and white or yellow flowers, catch and reflect even the smallest amount of light—they are good for dark rooms.

SHAPES AND TEXTURES

The style of a decoration is bound to depend to a great extent on the flowers available. People who are dependent upon the florist shop for supplies almost inevitably become accustomed to arranging a quantity of the same kind of flower simply because so many of the commercially grown kinds are either marketed in bunches or sold by numbers. These flowers are usually so well grown that they are perfectly uniform. They are also usually very stiff stemmed and have fine and healthy foliage. Because they are so well grown they are long lasting, but their very vigor, and certainly their uniformity, can cause some difficulty in arrangement.

A contrast of shapes and textures makes an arrangement more pleasing and sometimes much more distinctive than one of identical flowers. By studying this aspect of arrangement, gardeners and those who buy their flowers can add interest both to the flowers and to their assembly.

Often some of the materials from a previous arrangement can be held over and used in the next simply for the purpose of contrast. I have in mind things like gladiolus leaves which are long lasting and look well with other flowers. Even the stems of narcissus, cut on a slant after the faded blooms have been removed, can be used.

A contrast of texture is often easier for the city dweller to provide than a contrast of form. A few tall daffodils in a slim vase can 'wear' a posy of violets tucked in at the rim. Chrysanthemum blooms look well in front of boughs of thick-textured leaves. They also look good with strong grasses and rushes. Roses go with almost anything for they are classic flowers. Try them with branches thick with gray-green lichen. Narcissi look perfect with a few of their own contrasting leaves, but they are also in season with many lovely blossom boughs and young branches, such as catkins and pussy willow. Soft-petalled poppy anemones borrow liveliness from glossy Mahonia leaves. Ivy leaves particularly seem to suit the green centers of chincherinchees, while carnations seem to add glamour to any foliage whether it be simple laurel or exotic Dracaena.

A mixture of flowers needs to contain a contrast of shapes as well as textures. Arrangers who grow their own have the advantage here.

Uniform flowers can be given individuality by originality of design and by choosing distinctive companions for them. The hosta leaves are extremely long lasting and can be used time and time again. Even when they are fading they remain attractive.

Coalport china and *Cobaea scandens;* containers should not only be chosen with a room in mind, they also need to suit the flowers they hold.

Mainly about textures

Flower arrangers need a variety of containers to suit all flowers and settings. I have some favorite containers which I use time and time again at all seasons of the year, but even these do not suit all occasions. Large thick-textured blooms look ill at ease in fragile china, just as flowers with a delicate air may not suit thick pottery.

Not only do all highly distinctive flowers need suitable containers, but their companions need careful

choosing. One would not put fussy asparagus fern with calla lilies, rather I would use calla leaves. If no calla leaves were available, however, I would choose something of an equally strong character. Alternatively, I would rely on the design of the container and the style of the arrangement.

Where flowers have to be mixed you find that round flowers, chrysanthemums, carnations, zinnias and narcissi, for example, are enhanced by spicate forms. This means that containers used for short-stemmed, round flowers, if they are to be mixed with tall spicate forms, can be different from those employed if the flowers were arranged on their own. Spicate forms may be other flowers—gladioli, delphiniums or ixias—but they can also be grasses, rushes, reeds, leaves, blossom-studded stems, berry sprays, seed heads and ivy trails. Although we use the term 'flower' arrangement, in fact, any plant material that appeals to us can be used.

There is real enjoyment in discovering that a red cabbage is 'mighty like a rose', that the acid-yellow crinkly leaves of forced rhubarb have a coral-like texture and are much too lovely to throw away, that the rough skins of lychees accentuate the satin petals of white tulips.

(*Left*) The long bare stems of nerines and the delicacy of their blooms can stand strong contrasts. Thick-textured kale leaves anchor the stems to the modern glass dish.

(*Right*) Tall spikes of early-flowering gladiolus bring height, contrast and grace to shorter, uniformly stemmed, Super Star roses which they also match in hue. Pointed hosta leaves and ivy trails add contrasts of shapes and textures.

Decorations containing fruit and flowers can be quickly assembled. For this table decoration, hippeastrums, grapes, lychees, oak leaves and apples match the china.

Fruitful arrangements

Fruits are produced by flowers. Indeed, fruits are the whole purpose of flowers' existence so it is natural that they should look well together. Sometimes you are able to use the flower and fruit from the same family; roses and hips, nigella and its seed vessels, early cherries and plums, but more often fruits are as varied and as mixed as the flowers themselves. I use the 'fruit' here in its full botanical sense meaning the product of a flower, but for clarification let us now discuss the fruit we buy to eat.

All edible fruits are extremely attractive and can take part in home decoration. In fact, there are times when you are extra busy, when fruit will prove to be a great boon, for all you need are a few leaves, or other accessories and a flower or two and you can make an arrangement in a minute.

Then there are the other 'fruits', many of which can be kept indefinitely—pine cones and large seed heads of many kinds, such as lotus, poppy and magnolia. Some fruits last well but not indefinitely; these include gourds, berries, aubergines, peppers and fat, fresh seed pods.

As you learn more about plants you will find that you will

come to appreciate lovely leaves as much as lovely flowers. Often a flower arranger begins by treating leaves merely as something to put with flowers, but there comes a time when foliage begins to be featured prominently for its own sake.

Leaves are certainly as varied as blooms. Like them, there are some which can only be used fresh, but there are others which dry naturally or which may be preserved. When fresh leaves are to be used, some will need a little grooming. Evergreens, because of their long life, need cleaning. If the leaves are large it is simple to wipe over the surface of them. If they are meant to be glossy a final wipe with a clean tissue will help. A touch of olive oil will make them gleam.

Often a whole plant can be used such as a small cabbage, a rosette of saxifraga, succulent verbascum or Cryptanthus, or perhaps the center of a plant, such as the heart of the ornamental kale.

Ornamental gourds and squashes of all kinds are highly decorative, and if gathered when fully ripe and handled very carefully, they are long-lasting.

The delicate air of snowdrops belies their strength, for no flower which blooms at their season could be anything but incredibly strong. The glass which holds these seems to me to reflect their character. Its shape reminds me of the bulbs from which they grow.

CHOOSING THE RIGHT VASE

Previously I said that it was important for a container to suit the flowers and that it should also fit the occasion and the setting. To me, this really is important. A modern vase will look sadly out of place on traditional pieces of furniture.

For out flowers we need something which will hold water to nurture them; therefore, containers must be watertight or capable of being made so. Plastic bags and aluminum foil can be used to line any container you suspect might leak.

These may also be used when you want to protect a container from staining. I use them for metal and for some other containers I shall describe later.

I find that newcomers to flower arrangement tend to choose vases which are much too large, on the assumption that the flowers must have plenty of water, but if they are properly hardened this really is not necessary. It is much more important, certainly much easier and eventually more economical to choose a container which looks like it belongs in a room even when empty. If arrangements are to be placed above eye level, make quite sure that the container to be used is not so tall that it will be difficult to see what it contains. The wrong choice means that you see more vase than flowers.

When flowers are to be arranged on a dining-table, a similar point arises. Sit down at the table with the container in place and again make sure that it is not going to be too dominant and that the flowers will not be too high.

The style of arrangement will also influence the choice of container. Long, low arrangements may be better in narrow troughs rather than in wide bowls, if you intend massing the flowers. A tall vase will give length to stems, should this be necessary, because these will not have to reach the floor of the container.

(*Left*) Old-fashioned moss roses arranged in a brass tea-caddy. Many vessels originally designed for some other purpose are perfect for flower arrangements.

Bulb flowers like shallow water, so this scoop-shaped dish is ideal for gladioli which are very quickly arranged in this style. The 'dessert spoons' repeat the shape of the dish.

The lovely smooth glaze of this modern vase is matched by many flowers, but its pattern inspired the arrangement of hellebores.

Linking flowers with the container

All flower arrangers have favorite containers. They favor them for many reasons, but the most usual one is that the flowers seem to be arranged so much quicker and easier in them than in others. Quite a lot depends on how a stem holder can be fitted in. Sometimes a vase has an irritating shape to the rim and it is difficult to coax flowers to flow attractively over the edge. A tall vase with a fluted rim, on the other hand, often proves to be most agreeable. Many specially designed vases on sale seem hopeless and even a practiced arranger like myself can experience great difficulty in making a two-handled 'boat' vase, or an outsize egg-timer made of cut glass, look at all attractive. Because of this difficulty arrangers have turned to other objects which have proven to be esthetically successful.

Metal containers usually look good filled with flowers. Glass needs careful attention so that stems seen through the water look attractive and not messy. Patterned vases can be very difficult to use because the pattern really should harmonize with the flowers.

Generally speaking, plain colors are best. White and black are always safe; after all, they represent shade and light and your flowers will also be shaded or tinted. Any of the broken colors and their tints and shades also look good. Metal vases, also, can be classified as colors; brass as yellow, copper as orange, silver as white and pewter as gray.

Textures are important, but I think that these are more likely to be influenced by personal tastes. Choice of textures is usually the result of experiment and of practice, for after a time you will find yourself reaching automatically for a vase to suit, say, callas, cow parsley, rose hips or daffodils.

A container should be perfectly watertight otherwise furniture will become damaged. Some pottery needs a mat below it, which can be a nuisance. Alternatively, a sealing paint on the base of the container can be used.

Make sure that any containers you select will stand perfectly firm, as it is possible for them to overbalance when very tall stems are used. If they are opaque, this fault can be remedied by pouring sand in to weight the vessel.

Originally made as a glove box for a hall, the little drawer below this mirror now holds two gingerbread tins for use as flower containers.

Traditional flower containers

The reason why traditional containers are used less than they were is mainly because they are so difficult to use. The old method was merely to stand the flowers in the vessels with their stems reaching down to the bottom if possible. If we want to use any of these containers in the modern manner then we have to resort to modern means to do so. Church vases, for example, usually flute at the top and become narrow toward the waist. Flowers, therefore, need to be arranged mainly in the wide, top portion.

Arrangements in any vase of this type can be made to be attractive by arranging the center upright stem vertically. If this is also branched out flat, like beech for example, or if several stems can be mounted and fanned from a central stem like Cycas fronds, a large area of the arrangement is then filled. Other flowers or stems can then be arranged before this background.

The way that branch stems are cut or pruned can also ease arrangement in any tall narrow vase. If side stems are cut in such a way that a little of the main stem is retained this main portion can go into the vase and the side stem will still flow away from it, often at a right angle to it.

Pitchers have been used for centuries as flower containers but always for the bunch rather than for the arrangement. I

Carnations and nigella are arranged with silver-gray senecio foliage and phacelia; a bowl arrangement is still one of the most popular designs for decorating a table center.

(*Below*) Church vases are notoriously difficult to fill. One way of easing the task is to fill in the background with a flat, vertical but well-branching stem in front of which a few flowers can be arranged.

(*Above*) The simple pitcher is usually reserved for the unsophisticated bunch of flowers, yet it can also be used for arrangements in a more modern style as this one here.

think that jugs of all kinds are attractive, but if they are to be used for an arrangement certain points need to be explained. The handle of a jug is an important part of the design and I feel that it ought also to be part of the flower arrangement and should not be hidden. It helps, I find, if the contents are arranged in such a way that they appear to flow away from the handle. This means that curved stems will follow its curve—or roughly so. This rule applies to mugs, many of which make charming containers.

Extremely popular among flower arrangers are vases made in the style of the silver wine-coolers. I have used them for the humble yet graceful hedge parsley, as well as for great blowsy old-fashioned roses—no flower seems ever to be ill at ease in them. If you are lucky enough to own a silver cooler then use it for flowers.

Modern containers

The present interest in flower decoration has meant that all aspects of the art have been under examination. The Japanese have practiced flower arrangement for centuries, so long in fact that it is not the simple domestic but pleasant art that it is here. It is, instead, a highly sophisticated and ritualistic pastime. While the classic manner of oriental flower arrangement might not fit into our Western ways, certain aspects of it have a tremendous appeal and have influenced our own attitudes. One influence which has been most strongly felt is the oriental approach to the importance of the flower container. Eastern types are often very beautiful. Another aspect is the successful way in which only very few flowers are used in these containers. Western flower arrangers have been quick to learn the fundamentals of oriental design and have applied them to their own flowers. At the same time, a universal 'oriental' style, Ikebana, has captured a great deal

Cherry blossom and a Chinese bowl arrangement inspired by the Orient depends upon the beauty of a few stems in a lovely container.

of attention and this also has brought into popularity the shallow container.

This means that suitable containers abound but, once again, not all of them were intended as flower holders. Some of my own favorites are oven dishes, others are outsize ashtrays. And not all of them are modern. Some are deep plates, pewter as well as china. Small but deep trays are ideal for some purposes, especially when an arrangement of fruit is to be assembled. There are lidless china boxes. Anything deep enough to hold water or another supplementary vessel for water is pressed into service.

To use these particular containers effectively we have to realize that it is not intended that they should be filled with flowers in the manner of a traditional bowl but instead that they should provide an anchorage for them. The shallow container when used in an oriental style of arrangement is intended to be admired. It is as much a part of the arrangement as the flowers. The effectiveness of one is entirely dependent on the other. Invest in one or two well-designed dishes and there will be many times when you will find two, three or four flowers enough for a decoration.

Peonies and copper beech: well-designed shallow dishes help you to make three flowers and a few leaves play the part of many.

Black Wedgwood bowl is filled with marguerites, wheat, golden privet and wild vetch; the vase is modern and formal like the flowers and their arrangement.

The container often calls the tune! Modern glass, ceramics and metal vessels have clear lines and exciting shapes. They cry out for distinctive flower arrangements. Some people are so influenced by them that they have developed what I can only describe as 'pop' floral art in which the designs are either interpretive or abstract. I prefer to follow the style of the clean lines and to bring to these containers, flowers that either reflect their style or emphasize it.

When flowers are to be arranged in a mass, the container is of little importance. In most cases it is not intended that it should show, but when a beautifully designed vessel is used it seems a pity to hide it.

Take glass, for example. I love to see stems through water when they become magnified and seem to take on a new meaning and importance. However, stripped stems, on the other hand, are not pretty and if the outer skin of the stem has been damaged the water soon becomes cloudy. When I am using glass for roses, I do not remove the thorns from the stems because they are a gorgeous red under water.

Tall, slim containers, providing that they stand firmly, are useful to a person who wants to make a quick arrangement because one can use, say one gladiolus spike and a posy of leaves at rim level. Or tie a few flowers in the hand, their blooms at different levels and wedge in a vase with a few leaves.

Contrasting textures are effective. Leaves with rough textures look well against smooth but solid ceramics, as do woolly-leaved plants. I like to see narcissi arranged in a crescent, backed by their own leaves, and rising up either from a thick circular dish or a narrow, slightly blub-shaped vase.

(*Top*) Driftwood and 'ribbon' loops made from their leaves supplement and support narcissi in a Scandinavian glass jar. Stem ends cut from shortened blooms are also included.

(*Bottom*) A tall glass cylinder holds three nerines elegantly yet sufficiently. Their stems were tied together before arrangement, the calla leaves hide the tie at rim level. Leafless stems look lovely through glass.

Shallow containers

Arranging flowers is very much like painting, embroidery and sculpture. The flowers are our raw materials, our paints, thread or clay. Once we have learned a few fundamental rules about handling materials, the way we present them is not only a matter of skill and artistic merit but also personality. We can let flower arrangements speak for us.

If we are prepared to think of flowers as paints, it follows that we should be able to paint a picture with them. Some pictures will just be lovely to look at, like any flower painting, but others can tell a story, represent a theme, give a message, make a joke or even interpret an idea. Many people enjoy making arrangements of this kind but most of these arrangements are more suited to a flower show. However, if we are to tell a good story we need to use extra materials or accessories.

So far in this book the emphasis has been on flowers with passing mention of leaves and fruits, but the flower arranger should learn that there are many other materials which can be used. Anything which originates from a plant is acceptable. We have seen that leaves, stems and fruits can look lovely with flowers, but at times so can roots, bark, pith, husks and driftwood.

When we want to compose a picture or describe a scene, it is sometimes necessary to bring into it something which is not from a plant. This may also be natural in origin, such as a shell or stone but often a statue or some other little figure, a bird or butterfly perhaps, or even glasses, bottles, hats, boxes—any kind of object that has some relation to the subject, is used.

As I said earlier, this subject is to be dealt with more fully later but the reason it is mentioned here is because shallow containers are ideal for pictorial or scenic arrangements. In later winter you can lift many hearts by taking a prettily shaped branch and arranging it to represent a tree. Lay moss below it, stud this with the first tiny flowers to make a meadow in miniature. Or, in hot summer, cool the atmosphere with a low dish and an expanse of clear water, shell-strewn below; let a group of rushes rise from it and nearby let fresh green ferns lean out from mossy rocks.

(*Top*) Spring in Somerset: Alder catkin 'tree' towers above widow iris, primroses, daisies and toad-stools 'growing' on a mossy bank below.

(*Bottom*) A Christmas scene: Madonna and child with pine, holly, hyacinths and daffodils 'growing' from rocks arranged in a deep copper tray.

Brass-bound tea caddy, anemones, spindle berry, fuchsias and canary creeper—many boxes make delightful containers for unusual arrangements. Containers must be made watertight.

Wooden containers

It is not surprising that flower arrangements made in wooden containers look so delightful because wood is just one more of the many things which originate from plants. In recent years 'treen'—objects made from tree—have become extremely popular among flower arrangers in many parts of the world.

Technically, treen is manufactured, but occasionally you see a delightful arrangement held in a rough coconut shell or an outsize nut husk. On the other hand most treen objects are beautifully made. You can find tea caddys, bible boxes, skillfully turned bowls and occasionally a little vase. Many of these are antiques and because of this they need to be cared for very well if they are to be used for arranging flowers.

Water will ruin any of these containers and so precautions must be taken. Many tea caddys also contain little bowls which were once used to blend the tea and these are quite suitable for water but, even so, I would still line the caddy with aluminum foil in case any of the water should be spilled over the rim of the bowls.

A little vase made by a wood-turner and found in a junk shop holds a mixture of perpetuelles, cones, beechmast and leaves, pussy willow, honesty and grevillea.

If no container exists, then the piece of treen must be carefully lined with a double thickness of foil or plastic. It is also wise to use a soft foamed water-absorbent plastic stem holder such as Styrofoam or Oasis and not wire netting which might pierce the lining. Take care also to insert stems gently to avoid piercing.

Where the container has a lid, like the little tea caddy illustrated, it is easier to prop this open first before arranging the flowers. I usually take two pieces of stem, one on each side, to keep the lid lifted. You can then open the lid wide while the flowers are arranged and later lower it back onto the props.

I like to use a wooden container for a perpetual arrangement. These are described in a later chapter. In this case risk of damage to the container is far less because the stem-holding material is dry.

Certain flowers seem to look lovelier in well-polished wood than others, old-fashioned roses, velvety wallflowers, pansies, gloxinias and anemones are particularly appealing. A plywood, cylindrical, bath salts' container looks lovely with daisies!

Baskets are 'natural' containers

Like treen, most baskets are made from materials which have an affinity with flowers. Of course, I accept that modern baskets may be woven from man-made materials, but even then they follow traditional patterns which evoke a rural atmosphere. As containers for flower arrangements, baskets have never gone out of fashion, and they have been used since mankind first began to pick and offer up flowers to the gods and even now they are used mostly for celebrations.

The reason for this is mainly because flowers for special occasions usually have to be transported to the person or people who are celebrating a certain event. The special thing about a basket arrangement is that it can easily be carried without being disturbed.

This being the case, it really is most important that the handle should be left free enough to be held comfortably and in such a way that flowers arranged near it are not beheaded or damaged in some other way. When the flowers are being assembled, the handle should be considered part of the design. I usually treat it as a center stem. This subject is discussed in the chapter on styles of arrangement.

Like treen and other containers which may not be water-tight, baskets need some kind of lining. Some are sold ready lined with a removable tin container. Otherwise a lining must be improvised. If you use baskets for home flower decoration, (and incidentally a basket of flowers is really useful in a place where the decoration has to be moved).

An Easter basket of chick yellow mimosa, daffodils, and tulips is arranged around a 'nest' of gaily painted eggs. The basket is lined with aluminum foil. This is essential when a container is not water-tight.

You can use any vessel which happens to fit conveniently and fill it with water in the usual way. If the basket has to be transported, water which can be easily spilled is not practical and in such cases it is best to use a well-soaked foamed-plastic stem holder and to line the basket either with foil or sheet plastic.

Roses, candytuft, petunias and everlasting peas in a low basket make a pretty, yet practical, kind of decoration for a place where the arrangement must be moved from time to time.

For Mother's Day, violets, snowdrops and early viburnum blossom are arranged in a little basket lined with kitchen foil and packed with crumbled damp Florapak to hold and protect the frail stems.

An antique candy box is filled with cineraria blooms. Often a little assortment of flowers can be cut from a few plants without robbing them, to provide a splash of color when flowers are scarce.

A copper jelly mold with pinks, pansies, ornamental kale foliage and flowers and bunches of small red tomatoes makes a pretty and wholesome decoration for a kitchen. The lovely old mold is too attractive to hide away. The warm glow of the well-polished metal goes well with the gleam of the flowers and fruits.

Chincherinchees with magnolia and ivy leaves are in a glass bottle. Bottles come in all shapes and are often too lovely to throw away. Use them for flowers. The narrow neck is no problem if you first arrange the flowers in your hand and tie them in a slim bunch which is then easily wedged in place but do not forget to keep the water level up.

Parrot tulips, pansies and cabbage leaves are arranged in a copper skillet. The kitchen cupboard contains many vessels which are ideal for using in flower arrangement so why not borrow them from time to time?

A vase is filled with cornflowers, larkspurs, marguerites and Sweet Williams. You need never be at a loss for containers for there are many things around one that can be pressed into service with charming and attractive results. It is often surprising just what can be used.

Red anemones, a candle and pussy willow are arranged in a candlestick. Try a pair of these on the mantelpiece or arrange one at each end of a side table. Candlesticks make good pedestal vases and lift the flowers well out of harm's way.

Many flowers look well in shells. Not only is there a pleasant contrast of textures but often it is possible to color-link blooms and the container. In this picture, the conch is a tint of some of the mixed ranunculus it holds.

Here a modern china swan is arranged with narcissi. There are many pieces of bric-a-brac which make delightful containers for flowers. There seems to be an abundance of swans to be found among Victoriana and they are worth collecting. Try a fleet of them as a table decoration. Flowers need to be heaped like ruffled feathers to achieve the most effective result.

Build your own containers

Ingenuity plays an important part in flower arrangement especially where containers are concerned. Often you have a plan for an arrangement in your mind but the essential container is missing. There is usually a simple solution: build or make it yourself! It is surprisingly easy to combine one object with another to achieve the effect you want. Take a very simple example; take two matching egg cups of the traditional style, turn one upside down and place the other on it—result, a pedestal vase. Wrought iron can be fastened to a metal base and used as a pedestal. Two metal goblets can be joined in the way described for the egg cups. A bottle, or if you are planning a buffet table, a pair of them, can be supplied with a candle cup and used to hold flowers. Even an ordinary plate can be used as a base for flowers and fruit if it is first elevated in some way, but make sure that it is well anchored. A well-covered tin filled with sand, the same size as the vase will make a pedestal.

White tulips, *Cornus mas* blossom, ivy and deep-hued beetroot leaves in a fruit dish from the table china. Wine glasses hold more tulips.

Late Victorian clock sets do not seem to have much to do with flower arrangement, but parts of them are often to be seen both in flower shows and homes. The set usually consisted of a clock flanked on either side by a statuette cast in the same metal as the clock case. The statues are now often to be seen either as part of an arrangement or a composition.

If you want to elevate flowers there are many ways you can do so. For a large display take three bowls which may be either the same size or graded. In all but the top bowl, stand an empty flower pot and fit a bowl onto it. You can use more than one bowl if you want to make a tower of bloom. My table decoration of tulips shows a tower constructed on much the same principle except that wine glasses were used instead. Plasticine pills can be used under the glass base.

Usually, the main purpose of building an arrangement is to raise the flowers and you will find that many objects around can be used for this purpose.

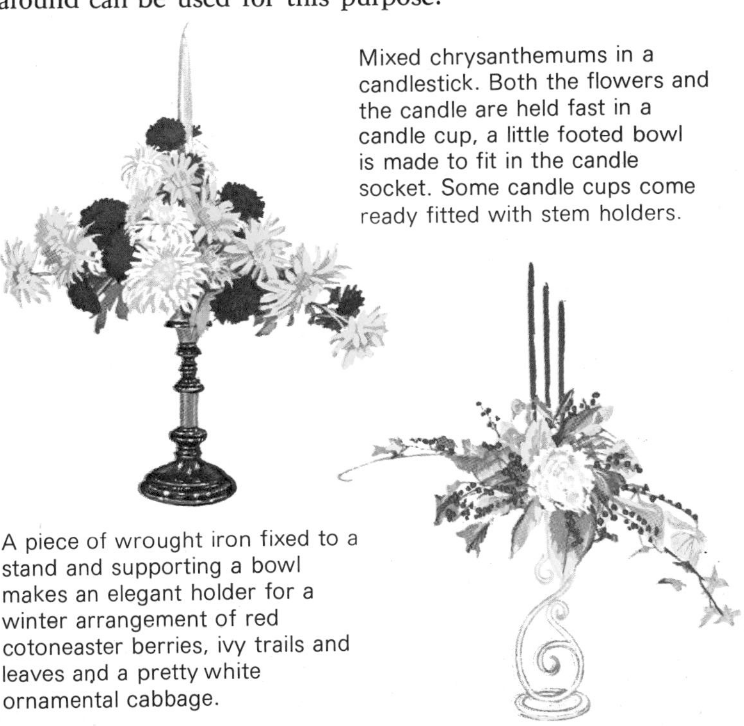

Mixed chrysanthemums in a candlestick. Both the flowers and the candle are held fast in a candle cup, a little footed bowl is made to fit in the candle socket. Some candle cups come ready fitted with stem holders.

A piece of wrought iron fixed to a stand and supporting a bowl makes an elegant holder for a winter arrangement of red cotoneaster berries, ivy trails and leaves and a pretty white ornamental cabbage.

A little white birch log has been hollowed out so that it will hold a Christmas decoration. The hole is lined with cooking foil and then packed with a cylinder of Oasis into which all stems can be inserted easily.

Roses and gypsophila are arranged in an antique pewter sugar scoop. Keeping stems moist is no problem today. Foamed urea, such as Florapak, will hold water and also keep stems well-anchored. There is no fear of drips damaging furniture surfaces.

Open work wicker baskets such as this which holds hellebores can be made quite watertight by lining them with foil or sheet polythene and using one of the foamed-plastic stem holders.

A modern wrought-iron candelabrum can be made to hold flowers if a block of Oasis is fixed on the center portion. This foamed-plastic, water-absorbent stem holder must be moistened daily because it evaporates more quickly being ex-container.

A tin can lid, nailed to a base on which pieces of driftwood have also been fixed, will hold sufficient Oasis to provide water for flowers so long as it is watered regularly to make sure it has not become dry.

An old-fashioned cutlery box divided into two compartments makes it possible to separate the flowers from the fruit. For the flowers the compartment is foil-lined. The stems are held in moist Florapak.

A tall glass supports a plate of fruit and flowers. There are a few anemones in the water held down by a tiny pinholder. Flowers among the fruit are in a block of Oasis hidden by kale leaves.

A pair of balances, whether real or a copy like these, makes an unusual side table decoration. Modern foamed plastics make arrangement considerably easier.

A conch shell holds the chrysanthemums which flow across the line of driftwood. Other shells and a sand-colored wooden base complete the composition.

GROUPING OBJECTS FOR EFFECT

When I described the purpose and the pleasures of making pictorial and scenic flower arrangements, I briefly explained the role that accessories can play and I mentioned a few of the most popular ones. We shall see later, when we come to discuss actual arrangement, that these can often play more than one part and that they can have a practical value as well as one which is purely decorative.

Meanwhile, we should not imagine that the accessories, no matter what they are, should be used only within the flower arrangement itself or that they are always arranged inside the container, for this is not so. Sometimes they play a more important and decorative part by being outside an arrangement. Yet because it is obvious that they have a purpose, they are seen as an essential part of a composition of related objects.

You will find, and I hope that my arrangements on this page show, that a grouping is often much more effective than a single vase. Do not imagine that composing a group is a complicated affair . . . but it is highly engaging.

One lesson a flower arranger soon learns is that it is not a bit of good planning a composition unless it can be practically translated. Not only must flowers stay in the required position, but everything else must also stay in place.

Much depends on how well things can be camouflaged. Napkin rings, pastry cutters or any other open ring can be used to lift and support many objects either in water or out. You can keep a pineapple in almost any position by using this method. It is also effective if you want to 'float' a flower in water. Flower pots, cream cartons and similar vessels will hold fruit or other objects. Several can stand inside each other.

Modeling clay holds many things in position but only if surfaces are perfectly dry. You can make small pills of the clay and fix these lightly to the base of any object to be held in place. Then press the object onto the place where it is to be anchored. The pills will flatten and hold. Or an alternative method is to roll out a length of clay, form it into a circle or oval and place the object to be held within it.

What could be more economical than this? Six daffodils, a cutting of Chlorophytum, which can be potted up when it takes root, and four lemons.

Look around you for inspiration

Once you become interested in composition you will find that ideas come fast, for inspiration is all around you. Take the china that you use every day for example. Study it to give you a theme for color or design. If it is a good shape, use it, though not necessarily as a container, for you may be able to use it some other way. A plate might make a good base for a low arrangement; a lid with an attractive pattern or perhaps an essential color can be used as a focal point.

Matching flowers with china is a useful, as well as an entertaining, exercise which you will find repays you well when you are looking for ways to decorate your table for a special occasion. I have more to say about this in my chapter on table decoration.

You might like to make a composition using some favorite object you own and linking it with flowers. A painting, for example, can be linked beautifully with flowers, fruits and leaves and some other accessory that will 'tie' them to the

Five white irises and a few stems of pussy willow are arranged with dried hosta leaves, gilded to match the rim on the willow pattern china.

Christmas decorations without flowers. (*Above*) A gloriously colored winter cabbage is the centerpiece of this composition. (*Right*) Christmas Tree decorations on false stems play the flowers' role in the tankard and add a little cheer.

painting. If your painting hangs over the fireplace, the mantelpiece will give a useful area for flowers. Otherwise you will need some other surface below the picture.

I collect shells and driftwood and I have an alcove in one of my rooms where a few shells are always on display. Here I enjoy making compositions that speak of the sea. It is surprising how many flowers and plants seem apposite, spiky daisies remind one of starfish, so do Cryptanthus and some other bromeliads; all rush-like leaves and sea-weed-like fronds play a part in setting the scene. Elsewhere I have a modern painting which reminds me both of a leaf and of an entire tree, of the soil and yet of the sky and here I tend to make compositions of treen, wood and wooden things such as hard, brown seek pods, leathery, preserved leaves, and fossil-thick oolite.

Flower arrangement is no static art. Once you learn the basic 'rules'—how to keep a stem in place and a flower long-lived—you can set off on a thousand journeys of discovery not only about nature and the world around you but also about your own creativity.

A base is an integral part of a design

Many people automatically place a mat under a vase of flowers, just as they do under a glass or beaker containing a drink, to prevent the surface of the furniture from being stained if the vessel is wet. Often these protectors are at variance with the arrangement in color, pattern, shape or in some other way.

A crocheted mat seems a long way from a beautiful stand holding an oriental arrangement, but there is a link. The Japanese place their flowers on a stand or base. In fact, this is often an important and integral part of the design and is known as 'dai'. But this stand also originally served to protect the polished surface of the little table or platform on which the flowers stood.

Because I am essentially a practical person, I look for practical applications in floral art and it is obvious to me that even with furniture that will not mark, or stem holders that will not spill water many arrangements are improved by being stood on a base. Displayed this way, an arrangement becomes 'lime-lighted'—your attention is drawn to it. From the purely practical point of view, a flower arrangement on a stand is often much more easily moved for dusting than a single vase, and from a further practical point, we return to the old question of economy, fewer flowers are needed for an arrangement displayed in this way because the base lends importance. It can also add color, texture, line and mood.

From the point of view of design a base often provides the extra little something which you feel is lacking in an otherwise pleasing arrangement. For example, even something as simple as a thick, dark circular mat can bring a seemingly too-frail arrangement to earth and give it a more stable quality. If you feel that your few flowers do not bring quite enough color you can add more by repeating their color, or alternatively, complementing it or harmonizing with it through the base.

From this you will see that not all bases are stands or platforms, although if you are lucky enough to possess one or more of these you are certain to find them useful at times. Bases, like so much else in flower arrangement, are really

what you make them—or perhaps it should be from what you make them! I have used plates, upturned ashtrays, a scroll of thick paper, the base of a Victorian glass dome, a plinth of a challenge cup, driftwood, slate, marble, trays and cake tins. But, remember, a base is not essential.

(*Above*) A base for flower arrangement can give importance to the design. It can also add color, texture, mood and style. The two bamboo mats under this simple yet lovely arrangement of just two chrysanthemums and jasmine leaves emphasize its oriental quality.

(*Left*) In most oriental styles the base is an integral part of a design. These roses are on the traditional 'dai' of the Japanese.

Peonies and the rough-textured, hollow stems of cholla wood are arranged on a large pinholder. Driftwood and a Billbergia plant hide the holder from view.

STEM HOLDERS

If you want to be able to arrange your flowers not only attractively, but also quickly and easily, it is vital that you should be able to assemble any kind of arrangement with confidence. The most important part of any flower arrangement, from the practical point of view, is the stem holder. Sometimes more than one is necessary; it all depends on what kind of arrangement is being planned.

If the stem holder is to be hidden within a container then we are not as concerned with its appearance. The main thing is that it should work. The cheapest and most efficient of all stem holder for this purpose is large-mesh wire netting. It is important that the mesh is large, one-and-a-half to two inches, because only the large size is malleable enough to be easily crumpled up and squashed into a container. Another point worth noting is that should a thick woody stem have to be inserted through the wire it passes through easily because if it pushes against the wire it will move it. Small mesh is much more rigid, and thick stems either will not pass through the small mesh at all or will be unable to influence it.

Short-stemmed carnations and roses are held secure by wire netting which fills the entire area. Long stems also may be arranged this way.

Stem holders should not be visible through glass. First arrange and tie the stems in your hand. Leaves or accessories added later can hide the tie.

Mesh used to be obtainable only as galvanized wire, but now there is plastic-covered mesh in black, green and white. It has the advantage of not marking the interior of precious china, but I think that it has the disadvantage of being a little slippery. This means that it may move on highly glazed containers until many stems are locked together. As the trickiest part of assembly comes at the beginning, this fault can be frustrating to a beginner. It also takes up a little more room in small containers because it is thicker. For large containers and for those which have a ridge at the rim which holds netting well, it is excellent.

If you store your containers you will find it best to keep the netting inside them after you have cleaned them. If you are afraid that it might mark the vase, store it in a plastic bag. As a general rule, the netting is cut to the size of the part of the container which holds the water, cut it twice its depth and match its width with the widest part.

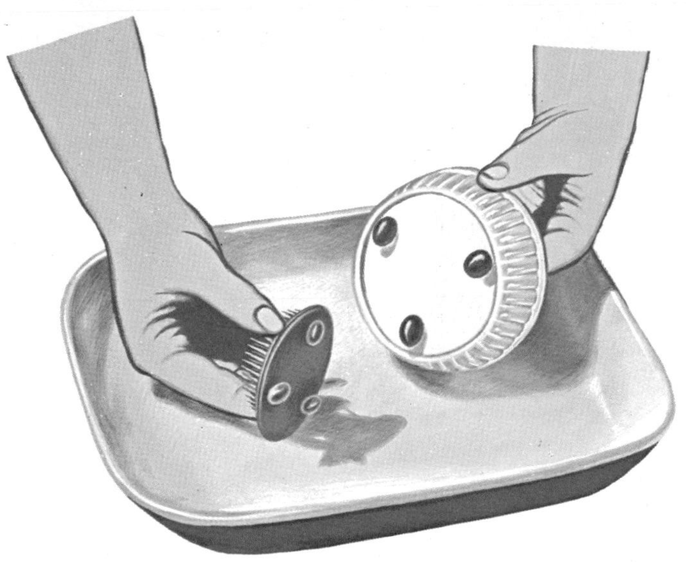

Pills of Plasticine make good washers and can be placed under any container or on a pinholder to secure one surface to another.

Tricks of the trade

There is no point in doing flower arrangement the hard way. You are sure to eventually discover a few tricks of your own, but meanwhile here are a few of mine.

I have found that the best way to fill a container with wire netting is first to bend it in a 'U' and then push it into the mouth of the vessel so that the cut ends of the netting are just protruding above the rim. These then can be curved over the rim to hold it firm.

Fasten netting high in glass

Florist wire lengthens short stems

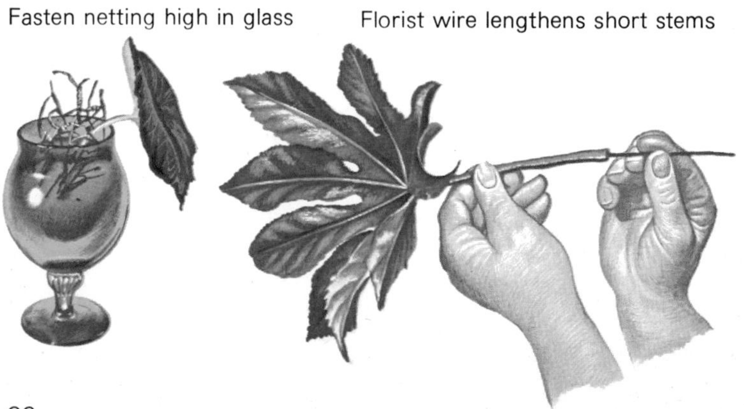

Cut ends will also help to hold very heavy stems in place especially if these are branched. As a rule the taller or heavier the stem, the more netting I use. At times this protrudes above the rim; but it is easily hidden later. The important point is that the netting can be taken around the lower portion of the stem in more than one place until it is as firm as a rock.

The snag ends are also useful in pinning stems in place. For example, you may need a low hanging leaf which will flow prettily over the rim, but it may be that the leaf has not really grown the way you want it. In this case a snag end can be passed around the leaf stem at rim level and then the wire—not the stem—can gently be bent so that the leaf reaches the point required. If you press hard on the stem you may snap it, but if the wire is bent, the stem it embraces is protected yet curves with it.

At other times the wire can be used just like a pin, by which I mean that a piece can be pushed through a stem at some point where it is necessary to hold it.

Although stems are held best if the netting fills the container from rim to base, this is not attractive looking when glass is used. Here the technique is to fix the netting in the top portion only and to make it shallow enough to be well hidden by the materials arranged lowest down. The plastic-covered netting I referred to earlier can sometimes be left in its original roll and fitted into the mouth of a glass. To arrange flowers on the side of a container, make a ball of netting, fix it on the side and pass the stems through.

Stem anchor

Stems inserted

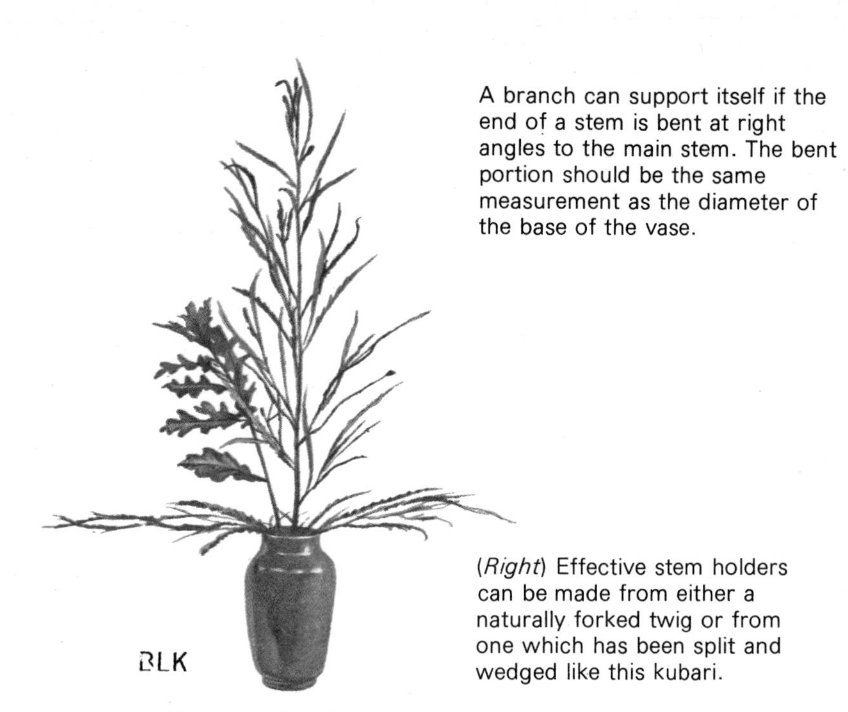

A branch can support itself if the end of a stem is bent at right angles to the main stem. The bent portion should be the same measurement as the diameter of the base of the vase.

(*Right*) Effective stem holders can be made from either a naturally forked twig or from one which has been split and wedged like this kubari.

Often one lovely branch is enough decoration in itself yet it is not always easy to arrange it if you rely on the support of the rim of the container alone. It is possible to wedge it firmly in a narrow-necked vase by pushing short thick pieces of bare stem between the branch and the vase. Another method is to use modeling clay pushed behind the branch. Patterns of other homemade stem holders can be borrowed from the Japanese who use forked and crossed sticks. They should always be cut from living twigs. Forked kubari—this is the Japanese term—can be made from naturally forked twigs by cutting the stems to the required length. Otherwise they can be made by splitting a piece of twig; Cupressus is excellent. Split twigs may need an extra piece of twig insterted in the fork so that the two arms remain apart. They may need to be held a distance apart by raffia or fine twine, or by using a rubber band to prevent them from springing open too far. Cross twigs are merely fastened in the center with raffia or fine twine.

The purpose of these holders is to prevent the branch from moving or to enable one to arrange a group of flowers

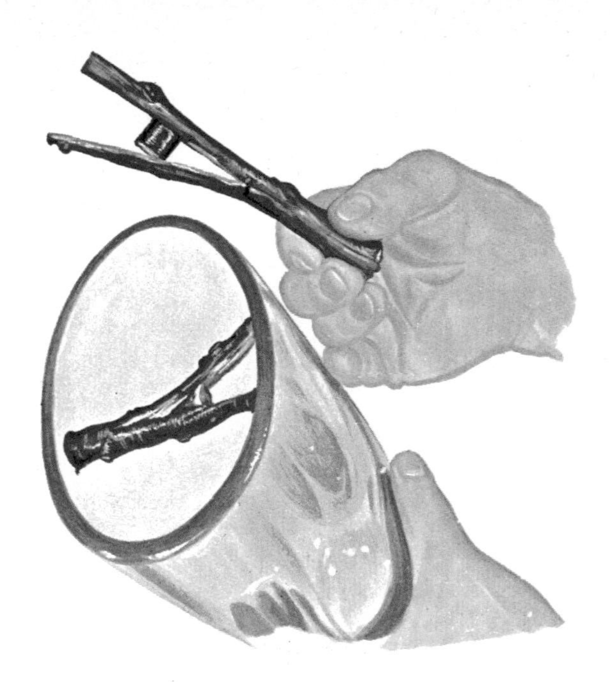

flowing at a required angle.

For very tall vases, an upright forked twig, standing a little higher than half the depth of the container can hold a leaning branch, the end of which is also forked. When the branch is arranged the end is fixed into the forked twig holder in such a way that only a small portion is actually in water as it lies across the container in a diagonal line.

Pinholders hold stems which are impaled on their points. Woody stems cut on a slant can be arranged at almost any angle. Very thick stems should be split for an inch and forked.

(*Below*) A small pinholder can be fixed to the side of a container by clay pills. Upright stems can then be pushed against the pin points where they will hold firm. They will also hide the holder from view.

(*Left and below*) A block of Oasis holds the mixed pinks and wild vetch arranged in a shallow container.

(*Above*) Oasis cylinders are joined together—the first stage in making this tall arrangement.

Foamed-plastic stem holders

When we look around us for new or unusual containers we see many which have an appealing shape, an interesting texture or perhaps a certain period charm and yet, they seem to be unsuitable mainly because they are much too shallow to hold water satisfactorily or in sufficient quantitites to keep stems turgid. At one time these would be passed by; today, thanks to the introduction of foamed, water-absorbent plastics, the range of containers and flower holders of all types has been greatly enlarged. I visualize the way in which I would like to display the flowers and then select the appropriate stem holder.

The plastics concerned are types of foamed plastic. The important thing is their texture—soft, sponge-like and unresistant. You can insert a stem and, if the flower is only a short one, you need push in no more than an inch of the base (which obviously is a great advantage), and it will hold quite firm even if you turn the block of plastic upside down.

Because the plastics absorb and hold water they can be used for arrangements which have to be stood on polished

(*Right*) A block of Oasis holds this carnation tree.

surfaces where spilled water would cause damage.

They are divided into two types. One, Florapak, should be used inside containers. It can be used time and time again, but as more stems are inserted and taken out the material crumbles. I find that the crumbled mass can be pressed down to compact it and a new piece laid over it. The other, much firmer, Oasis, keeps its form and so can be used without a container.

Florapak holds water for a long period because it is not exposed. For this reason it is ideal for arrangements which have to be placed out of reach. Even so, plants which are very long lasting take a lot of moisture and so the water should be replenished where necessary.

Oasis, on the other hand, because it is used ex-container loses water quickly and needs soaking afresh each day. The exception is when the Oasis block is held in a vessel into which some water can be poured, as in the urn base shown on the opposite page. The moisture will then be taken up by capillary action as the block dries.

Attractive ways to hide stem holders

In many ways it is a good thing that a pinholder in a low dish or other type of container should have to be hidden because the way you decide to camouflage it can add to the interest of the arrangement as a whole. Hiding the stem holder often anchors the flowers in a way that really makes them and the container become one unit. Whatever you use should bear some relation to the flowers. Sometimes all you need is one large flower from the group which forms the arrangement with its stem cut short so that, as it leans out from the holder, either it or the leaves which grow close to it, hide the stem holder completely.

At other times other accessories are needed, and it really is worthwhile building up a collection of stones, shells, small but broad and well-shaped pieces of driftwood, cork, bark and any natural material that appeals to you, so that you can always find something which will suit the flowers you are using. All of these things are so diverse that you are sure to find some to blend with all containers.

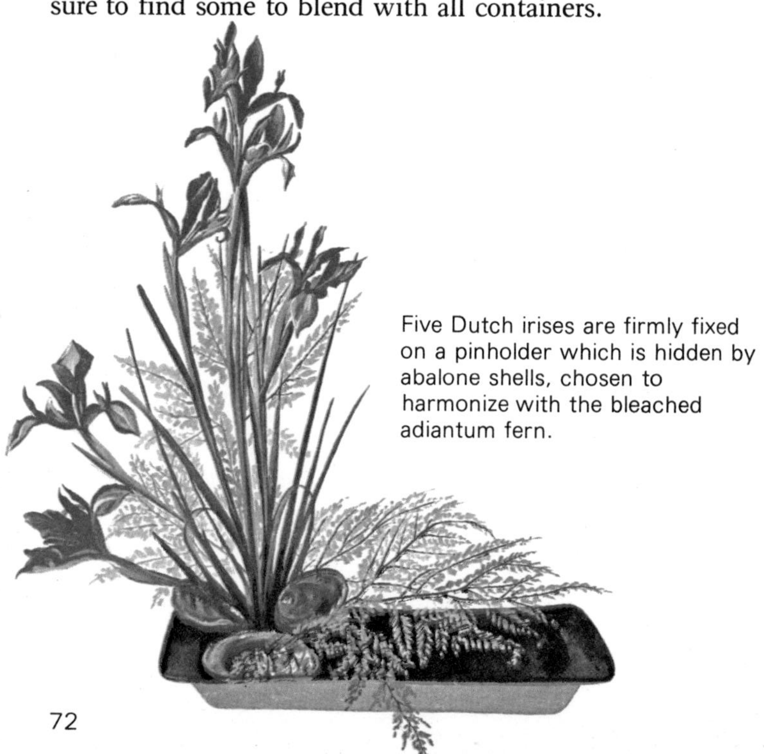

Five Dutch irises are firmly fixed on a pinholder which is hidden by abalone shells, chosen to harmonize with the bleached adiantum fern.

Fruits of all kinds are useful for hiding stem holders. Most will have to be kept out of water otherwise they are likely to spoil. There are several ways in which this can be done. Any Oasis blocks, with their bases covered in foil so that they do not draw up the water and become wet, can also be used. These also can be stacked or halved to give different levels if necessary. The fruit can either be pressed into the plastic and thus made to stay in place, or it can be mounted on a false stem which can then be held secure by the Oasis.

Often it is quite simple to lay a piece of bark, wood, or cork mat, or even a piece of small-mesh wire netting, or folded large mesh, across the container from one side to the other at the foot of the flowers, and to arrange the fruit on this. One advantage of netting is that it can be shaped to fit in between stems and the rim of a container. It can also be curved easily so that, should this be necessary, it can follow the shape of a container. It can also be molded to form a bowl or a trough to take fruits of all shapes and sizes.

Assorted gourds hide the pin-holder on which these hippeastrums are held. Together with the flowers and autumn leaves they match the container's colors.

Three formal dahlias with richly colored ligularia leaves, which supplement the flowers, furnish and color-match the bowl, and hide the stem holder.

Leaves as stem holders

Often one of the quickest, most practical and, at the same time, prettiest ways of hiding any kind of ugly stem holder is by leaves, which can also form an important feature of the arrangement.

There are so many lovely kinds of foliage which can be used and even if you have no garden, often you can use the leaves from the flowers you buy. Look over stems before you strip them to see if there are not some extra good samples which will do, if not for one arrangement then maybe for another. Lay them carefully one on the other and stand them in water until you are ready for them. Many leaves, such as those of gladioli, bulbous irises and daffodils seem only to be useful for tall arrangements when their contrast of shape can be exploited, but actually these can also be used at low levels if they are first looped and arranged in 'ribbon' bows.

Some of the leaves which cry out to be used because they are so lovely may not generally be considered to be flower arrangement material, but they will cover a holder very nicely. These include the outside leaves of winter cabbage, which are often tinged with lovely hues, the yellow leaves of forced rhubarb, raspberry, strawberry, celery and many other humble plants.

Town dwellers should keep a lookout when walking in the park in autumn for many of the fallen leaves can be pressed, oiled and used again and again. It is wise to collect many kinds and store them flat in plastic bags until they are to be used. Evergreens are extremely nice when used in this way.

Leaves should be gathered with stems (petioles) as long as possible so that they can be easily arranged. Those for pin-holders need only to be impaled on the points or laid across them but those which are to flow over the rim of deeper containers may need a little help. It is often quite easy to insert a florist wire up the fleshy petiole either to the margin of the leaf or just far enough to hold firm. The protruding portion can then be inserted down into the wire netting or other stem holder. Alternatively, pipecleaners can be twisted around the base of the petiole to elongate it and to make it easier to arrange.

Tall crown imperials are in a matching vase which is filled with stem-holding large mesh wire netting. Fatsia leaves are artificially elongated by wires inserted in the stem ends.

STYLES OF ARRANGEMENT

Personal tastes play as important a part in the art of flower arrangement as they do in other visual arts. The style of decoration favored will depend upon what kind of flowers you like to grow or buy. These will be (or ought to be) influenced by the colors of your interior decoration. Also, the flowers are likely to influence not only the choice of the type of container used, but also the setting in which the finished arrangement is placed. And, of course, the flowers must suit their surroundings.

Certain people want to be completely surrounded by flowers. Take, for example, the man or woman whose hobby is growing chrysanthemums, dahlias, gladioli, roses or some other specialist flower. Such people often have dozens of plants which yield many hundreds of flowers all destined for cutting. Such enthusiasts will not be interested in a few blooms, arranged in oriental styled designs!

But not everyone has masses of flowers or wants to have so many around him.

An arrangement is often more likely to be an ornament than a true flower piece. Here the line of the complete ensemble was designed to fit a certain scene and to bring to it a touch of color and a hint of atmosphere.

Shrub roses are arranged in a simple manner in a modern but traditionally styled Wedgwood vase. This free, loose bunch style is especially suitable for old-fashioned garden flowers like these.

Modern flowers look well arranged in the modern manner. As most flowers grown from bulbs and corms last best in shallow water there is a further advantage in choosing a style such as this for gladioli.

There are those who prefer to see just a few flowers esthetically displayed. There are others who lead such busy lives the leisurely flower arrangement is either impossible or a seldom indulged luxury. These people tend to look on flower arrangement from a different viewpoint than those I first mentioned. But there are methods of easy arrangement for them as well, and later these also will be explained.

The lover of pure flower decoration is often puzzled by the stark simplicity of modern floral art and claims that this has nothing in common with the traditional manner of displaying blooms. Inevitably, we find that the term 'flower arrangement' is too restricting and does not satisfactorily describe all the forms of floral art we see. Yet there is no other term for it, and we use it whether we are thinking in terms of putting roses in a jug, building a cone of seed heads, arranging a piece of driftwood with a succulent plant or filling an altar vase.

Arrangements of informal flowers like these clustered floribunda roses can be used in many ways according to their size and content. These were to decorate a long table.

Formal or informal table settings

Once, to do the flowers meant little more than arranging a few choice blooms in a vase designed to hold as much water as possible. Modern arrangers find old-fashioned vases very difficult to use which is one reason why containers not originally made to hold flowers are used.

Styles fall roughly into two groups, formal and informal. These groups are also subdivided, as we shall see. The type of flowers often, but not always, dictates the group into which their arrangement falls.

Generally speaking you will find that, since commercially produced blooms have to be as perfect and as uniform as possible, these tend to fall into formal styles when they are arranged, even if the arranger was not following a well-defined theme.

On the other hand, most flowers which are allowed to grow in a perfectly natural way, by which I mean not disbudded, staked or trained, tend to fall easily and happily into informal styles. A suitable choice of both stem holder and container increases this informality and results in a charming arrangement. Yet it is possible to arrange even the most unsophisticated flowers, the species rather than the man-made hybrids, into an informal design.

After many years I have learned that you can let flowers work for you. Informality is easily achieved when simple flowers grown quite naturally are used. They usually want to go their own way, and the wise arranger allows this. So far as shop-bought flowers are concerned, you may find, as I do, that their perfect uniformity is often best exploited. They can be arranged in highly formal and sophisticated designs and look quite wonderful, often much more distinctive than if they had been reduced to an artificiality by having been smothered with softening agents like fern.

Formality exploited! These uniform narcissi are arranged in a long curve by shortening stems to different lengths. Later the cut ends are also arranged.

Using your individuality

Except when we are arranging flowers for exhibition and competition there is really no reason at all why we should not arrange flowers exactly as we like. If we have personal tastes why should we not express them.

At this point I feel that I should stress that I, personally, am not attempting to dictate how *you* should arrange *your* flowers. Instead, I am endeavoring to tell you how I do mine. I also believe that if, on the other

Formal flowers, like these daffodils, often strongly individualistic, need to be arranged with both skill and understanding.

hand, you conform and accept or adopt the present popular styles of arrangement you can use them also as a means of self-expression. I make the plea that as you learn to arrange flowers efficiently you are not content to copy but strive to develop a style of your own. You will find it a rewarding experience.

My own first experience with making individual flower arrangements was with daffodils. For years I had arranged these flowers in a simple pitcher or mixed them with spring blossom in a vase, but one day, confronted with several almost identical bunches of flowers I decided to make some arrangements quite different. I hit on the idea of 'stepping' the stems, cutting each a different length so that every bloom could be displayed, and then standing them on a pinholder in a shallow dish.

Since that time a simple curve of formal flowers has become one of the accepted styles, and one is likely to see many adaptations of it at all times of the year.

In this winter decoration, the orange-hued Galaxy chrysanthemums are matched by the undersides of the distinctive leaves of *Rhododendron Falconeri.*

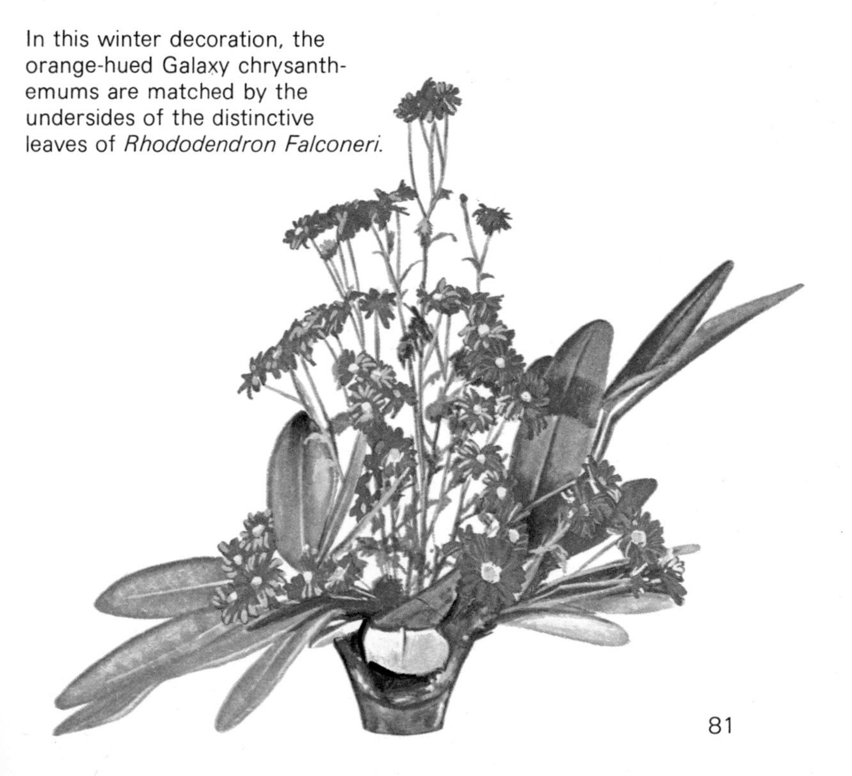

Traditional flower arrangement tends to fall mainly into a few patterns based on certain shapes. This, roughly a half globe, is one of them.

Traditional patterns

Patterns which have been in vogue for many decades, even centuries, have a right to be called traditional. They are based on the simple bunch which was once placed in water, as it was, with the stems still bound. One can imagine that a round posied bunch would be stood on a low table where it could be properly admired and that a tall bunch, or a sheaf, would be stood in a taller vessel with its back to the wall.

Then flower arrangement became more sophisticated. Instead of being bunched they were arranged individually, yet the old patterns were still followed. In a bowl, flowers were

Even when loosely arranged and informal in character, many designs are fundamentally traditional. In this mixture of sweet peas, pinks and roses the pattern, once again, can be described as a portion of a globe, as an outline around the outer stems will show.

arranged to represent the round dome of the posy. The sheaf shape, which traditionally was made with some protective green fern fronds at the back, was repeated in side vases.

We have never really broken away from these old styles mainly because there is nothing which quite replaces them. Also, flowers tend to fall into these patterns themselves.

I think that it helps the arranger to study natural plant shapes and in the imagination to convert them into styles for flowers using their proportions as a guide.

There are just a few shapes that are continually repeated. The pyramid or cone is to be seen all around us and there are many variations played upon this theme from the stylized spruce pyramids to the slim leaf shapes of the cypress. The globe which we have seen in fruits of all kinds is halved along its equator when it forms a bush. As these are nature's own shapes what is more natural than that we should have taken them as guides for our own art forms?

An arrangement designed to be placed against a wall needs a flat back. It is, in effect, a bunch or sheaf, with stems hidden by the vase.

A table center for Christmas based on the posy theme. It has chincherinchees and chrysanthemums on a circular base of green.

Arctotis and pansies are set in a wide-angled triangle which enables one to make a wide band of color with only a few flowers.

Hybrid tea roses fall beautifully into globular or semicircular designs which repeat the outline of the flowers themselves.

For a winter arrangement, a few pruned stems of eucalyptus contain within their pattern three tulips and three lilies-of-the-valley. The figure three is used here to emphasize the triangle theme.

Pink and blue chicory make a triangle of color around an inner triangle of kale leaves, framing pompon chrysanthemums and pineapple mint.

In this summer arrangement of peonies, sweet peas, delphiniums, pinks and spiraeas the flowers are arranged in almost an entire globe.

The triangle is a favorite pattern in flower arrangement. Here, the lichen-covered twigs are set in a triangular-shaped pattern and the one chrysanthemum and gourds are placed within their outline.

Even large flowers like dahlias can be arranged in a posy. Here with pungent yellow fennel, they are arranged in a copper mug to decorate a kitchen dresser.

(*Above*) The first stems to be arranged are the center one, which defines the height, and the two side stems at roughly right angles to it which define the width of the arrangement. The intermediate stems should never be taller than the center or the proportions will be unbalanced.

It is important that no stems are seen to cross but that each one appears to flow out from a main center source at the foot of the center, vertical stem.

Variations on a theme

In spite of the great variety of flowers and plant materials we use, most of them fall very easily into traditional shapes based on the globe, semicircle and circle. They are often very elegant.

If an arrangement is to be viewed from all points, the stems should radiate from the center in all directions, but if it is to be faced one way, like the arrangement illustrated, they need only flow in a semicircular sweep, radiating from the center stem.

I would say that of all the styles or patterns of flower arrangement, those which are based on the globe are the most useful.

This all-round arrangement, as it is often called, is a basis for so many decorations as we shall see when we come to the next chapter.

A true cone, by which I mean a pointed shape or a round base, is also useful, but tends to be more formal than the rounded shapes. Flowers are easily arranged in this pattern, and it entails only a simple matter of changing the lengths of the stems. The central stem, which goes into place first, should be very much taller than the side stems. The shorter the side

Pyrethrums and sweet peas in a circular pattern are really a section of a globe split down the middle. Their tips make almost a full circle.

stems are and the greater the difference between them and the center stem, the more pronounced the shape of the cone will be.

If an arrangement has to be spreading, say a low bowl close to the table's surface, then the central stem must be much shorter than the side stems. Again, the way they are cut and arranged will make the arrangement either conical or circular.

One thing is most important and this is that all the stems should appear to be radiating from a common source at the very center of the arrangement. This they cannot do practically, but if every one of them leans away from the center stem, the only vertical one, they will give this effect.

Flowers for the table

Down through the ages there have been many occasions when table decorations have been extremely elaborate although their original purpose was simple enough. In Roman times, for instance, certain flowers were thought to be efficacious in warding off drunkenness. For this reason they were generously (and thoughtfully) heaped in front of the guest known to be bent on enjoying himself to the fullest. Roses were said to be particularly good for this purpose, so much so that these flowers were often made into garlands and given to a guest to hang around his neck as he sat down to wine and dine. Sometimes the wreaths were placed on the table instead.

Other flowers were said to ward off fever, and for this reason sweet-smelling kinds were highly valued. These flowers, with sweet smelling leafy herbs were made into posies, sometimes called tussie-mussies, and placed on tables about the house. When a special guest was to be entertained, the posies would be somewhat larger and consequently sweeter than usual. Sometimes there would be many on a table, one for each guest. So customary is it that to many of us a table does not look complete unless flowers are set upon it, even if it is otherwise bare.

In the home, flower arrangements on the table should add to the intimacy and friendliness of the occasion, but this has not always been so. There have been times when, after the first gasp of wonder or surprise, they must have been more intimidating than otherwise. This was, as one might expect in Victorian and even on into Edwardian times, when flower arrangements literally reached great heights. I understand that the purpose of such ostentation was to add to the general effect of beautifying the room and that they should be visible over the heads of the guests. Now table decorations should be low so that they do not form a screen between one person and another. They look best if they harmonize with the table linen and china and will be more pleasing during mealtime if they are not heavily scented.

An example of a Victorian table decoration taken from a contemporary magazine.

A far cry from Victorian opulence—Leek flower heads, lupin, poppy and honesty seed heads and mixed foliage match modern china.

The candle is the main 'stem' in the Christmas decorations above.

Methods of arrangement

As I said earlier, the 'all-round' arrangement is a good basic shape and lies at the root of many designs which can be as varied as a large decoration on a pedestal to grace a great hall or a table decoration for a small Christmas party.

The most important stem is the central one. It is well worthwhile spending a little time on this to ensure that it is both properly placed and well anchored so that no stems arranged later will be likely to move its position.

If candles are used, they should be treated as flowers or

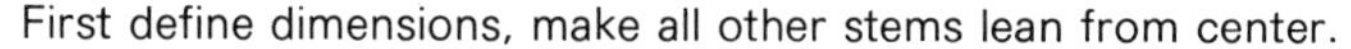

First define dimensions, make all other stems lean from center.

(*Above*) Imaginary axis. (*Above right*) Flowering stems.

stems. One candle should be set in the center and all subsequent stems should radiate from points around its base. If two candles are used you should imagine that the central space between them is the axis of the arrangement. This way lines and proportions will be pleasing.

Candles are easily arranged. Wire netting will support them quite well although you may have to hold them erect while the first few stems are arranged. These will soon wedge them in place. I use a combination of styrofoam or Oasis, and place the netting over and around this. The base of the candle then goes through the upper layers of netting and down into the plastic where it is held firm.

If you want to arrange a candle on a pinholder, first warm the pinholder by standing it in hot water. The candle will then fit easily on the points, but do not forget to make the pinholder base quite dry again before fixing the clay pills on it. Remove the candle in the same way.

If using a basket with a handle, you should take this into consideration. Decide where the center point lies, and if it is not possible to stand an upright stem under it, and this will depend upon both the style of the basket and how high the handle stands from the container, then imagine an axis immediately under the center of the handle. Arrange the stems so that they radiate from this.

If you want to build an arrangement using two or more bowls, one above the other, determine the center of the top bowl and imagine it extends to the center of the lower bowl.

To celebrate a Golden Wedding, this little bowl contains some very straight stems, but natural golden foliage and ribbon bows bring a soft touch to them.

If the tip of the center stem is directly over the center of the base of the container, the arrangement will always be well balanced no matter how mixed the components. Side stems at wide angles to the center stem will flow low and add an informal note.

A raised container brings grace to a bowl arrangement, especially if the stems of some components are stiff. It also allows the arranger to use short-stemmed materials.

When a little informality is required, place the center and side stems in position first.
The following stems need not 'sketch' a formal outline. Instead cut them and group them at varying levels, recessing some of the larger blooms.

A pineapple of carnations with croton leaves and Christmas tree decorations is arranged for a party table. Here the stems are short but the principles of arrangement are the same as for the longer stems seen here.

Formal and traditional, chrysanthemums are arranged in a silver punch bowl. Spray flowers are sometimes so clustered that the stem for the center needs thinning or it will look top heavy.

An all-round arrangement is not necessarily one held in a low bowl. This little shell-shaped container held by a dolphin raises short-stemmed pansies and pinks so that they may be easily admired and smelled.

When mixed shapes are used, they often look attractive if they are grouped in their kinds or colors. However, if this is done, do not separate the zones too severely but allow them to merge one with another.

An arrangement placed at the end of a table can be tailored to fill the space by extending or shortening the side stems as required.

Obviously, where table settings are concerned, a great deal depends upon the size of the table and the number of guests to be seated around it, but if we realize that we do not have to be restricted to a plain bowl in its central area we are much more likely to devise original and pleasing decorations.

Take, for example, the small room in which one end of the table is often flush against a wall. If the decoration is placed at this point it will not only look very attractive, but you will find that its site is also practical. The rest of the table will be clear for china, glass and linen.

If you choose this position you can place a long arrangement made to measure, or a triangular design almost flat against the wall. Pairs of arrangements look well in this position, and you will find that decorations made in candle cups look appropriate. Tiers of flowers, or fruit and flowers mixed, can flank a central mass of fruit. One advantage of this particular kind of placement is that the flowers are never likely to impede the guests' view!

What about free-standing tables? Sometimes two or more arrangements running the length but leaving the actual center clear are more convenient than one main bowl, for then an area is left free for fruit or some other dish. When you do this, take care none of the flowers stands too high.

Arrangements running across the table diagonally divide the table in a very nice fashion. This line need not be dense with flowers but can be determined by foliage, ivy trails for example, superimposed with troughs of flowers according to the size of the table and the importance of the occasion.

On a really large table, flowers at varying heights look very attractive especially if the lower-stemmed ones in the taller decorations are brought down to touch, or almost touch, those at a lower level. Sometimes the difference in levels can be effectively accentuated by candles. Study the pattern and colors on both china and table linen so that you can select plant materials to harmonize.

Often two or more arrangements look prettier than one bowl, especially if they are placed diagonally, leaving room in the center.

Flowers which carry their blooms at an angle to their stems are known as 'faced' flowers and are ideal for arrangements designed to face into a room.

Flowers to face into a room

There are many places about the home where flowers may be displayed against a wall and, in this case, it will be much more convenient (and, as we shall see, economical) if they have flat backs. Yet, even if this is so, the arrangement itself should never appear flat and contourless.

Most formal arrangements could be said to be all-round styles sliced down the middle. Thus, we can have a half cone which will appear to be triangular in outline and a half globe which will have a circular or a semicircular shape. With only these two important shapes, we can have many lovely variations.

The only real difference between these styles and the all-round designs we have been discussing is that all the action, as it were, is only on one side of the arrangement. However, if you take the idea of an arrangement down the center too literally, you are likely to find that the finished design may be too flat-backed to be pleasing. It all depends on where it is to stand in the home but, beware, it may look

An arrangement with a flat back is ideal for floral mixtures. Tall graceful stems can be used to provide height, while smaller-stemmed flower masses can be used low down, centrally, at rim level or even lower.

unattractive when viewed from the side. It is important that such arrangements should always look well in profile. Fortunately, this is something which can easily be done.

Even though, in a sense, we halve the mass of flowers, there is no need to halve the area of container in which their stems are to be placed. So, if when we begin assembling them we take the tallest vertical stem and, as before, place it in the center of the arrangement but, instead of also placing it in the middle of the container, we take it back as near to the rim as possible, we shall leave almost all the area of the container to be filled. Then we can arrange the following stems in the same way as before, allowing each one to lean away gradually from the central vertical stem which defines the height of the arrangement.

As work proceeds, look occasionally at the profile of the arrangement and view it as it might be seen by, say, someone entering a room.

Often you need no more than a leaf or a short spray flowing over the back rim. Sometimes it will be necessary to take the flowers around more than the 180° of a half circle.

Containers are important

Once again, we realize that an attractive arrangement does not depend solely upon the flowers. As I have stressed before, while it is by no means important that they should be valuable, containers need to be chosen with care. For example, a stemmed or pedestal vase will lift short-stemmed flowers and give them an air of elegance and importance. Many gorgeous short-stemmed blooms are ideal for massing at rim level in mixed designs.

Many of the mass-produced flowers bought from the shop have very straight and stiff stems which often offer problems to the flower arranger. A pedestal vase will help dispel any over-stiff effect. The tulips in the arrangement illustrated here have straight stems which are unlikely to curve much in water, but both the container and the twigs behind them have helped to make them look a little less formal. One advantage a pedestal vase has over deep, tall ones is that you do not need many flowers to fill it.

It is important that the flowers and their container should not only belong to

Many of the flowers in this arrangement: pansies, scabious, snapdragons, sweet peas and petunias are short stemmed, but the pedestal dolphin vase raises them gracefully.

This little footed vase which so nicely matches the color of the ivy and tulip foliage brings a dignity to a dozen short-stemmed double tulips.

each other but should be seen to belong. By this I mean that not only is it important to select a container which suits the flowers in size, color and texture, as we have seen, but that it and the flowers should merge.

This is not at all difficult to achieve. If you study the illustrations on these two pages you will see that in every one, flowers and other materials arranged more or less at rim level and below it, have been made to flow out over and below the actual rim. This way they eliminate any hard and well-defined line which might otherwise exist.

This effect also serves another purpose, for by bringing the flowers out over the rim you make the arrangement greater in depth at its base. This improves its profile.

Again, you will see that all the stems do not flow out over the rims for the same distance. Some, like pansies, ivy clusters and forget-me-nots, are much shorter than the others.

If flowers are allowed to flow out and below the rim of a vase, an arrangement becomes well integrated; but these flowing stems should not be of equal lengths.

Styles unlimited

There is really no limit to the styles you can choose for arrangements to stand against a wall or in some other place where it is not essential that they shall be viewed from all angles. whether these are formal or informal will really depend as much upon the flowers and other materials as upon the type of container and the nature of the setting in which the arrangement is to be placed.

Generally speaking, mass-produced, uniform flowers tend to fall into formal patterns. They can only be made to look informal by using certain accessories. Actually, a great deal of entertainment and pleasure can be derived from trying to create an informal scene from seemingly unsympathetic materials.

If time is important to you it might be wisest and best to compromise. Begin by having a selection of containers that will suit florist flowers. Devise a pattern of arrangement which appeals to you and which you can carry out quickly and easily. Do not think that uniformity is necessarily monotonous.

Remember that the formal styles are symmetrical and are

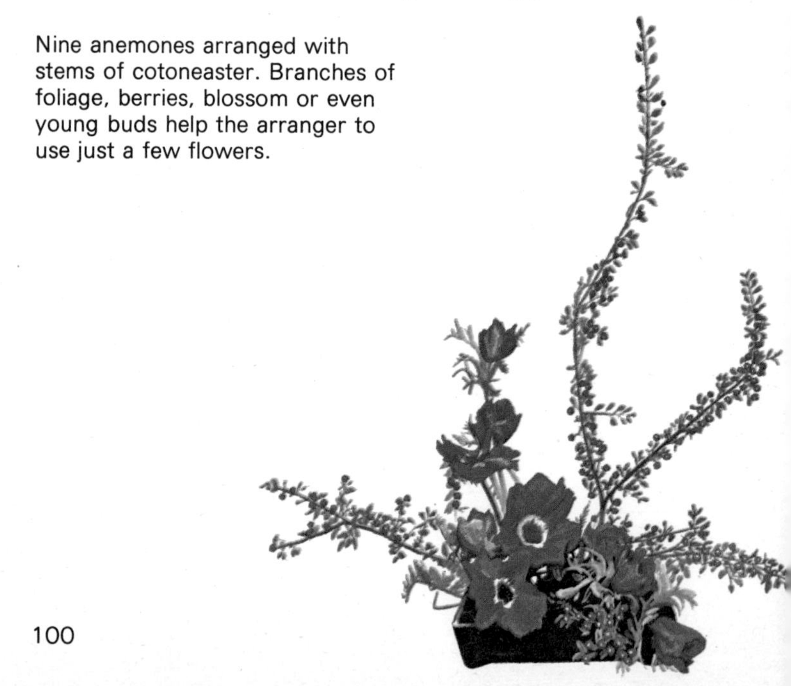

Nine anemones arranged with stems of cotoneaster. Branches of foliage, berries, blossom or even young buds help the arranger to use just a few flowers.

fundamentally based either on the globe or the cone. Take the triangle for example. Nothing is easier than to arrange six uniform flowers into a triangle merely by shortening the stems so that beginning at the tip, you have one, two (one on each side of it at a lower level) then, one again, in the center and lower than the two side flowers; and then two, as above but leaning just a little farther out. If the flowers are well supplied with their own foliage the arrangement might be complete, but it is more likely that it will be improved by some complementary material arranged within the line of the triangle.

If you exercise your imagination you will find many ways of using just a few flowers even for a large arrangement. A flat branch of beech, spruce, pine or maple, for example, can be placed at the back of a container so that it forms a triangle or semicircle defining the size and shape of the finished arrangement. Lower or misplaced side stems should be trimmed away and rearranged to flow over the rim or set aside to arrange later among the straight-stemmed blooms. The backcloth of foliage will help eliminate their formality.

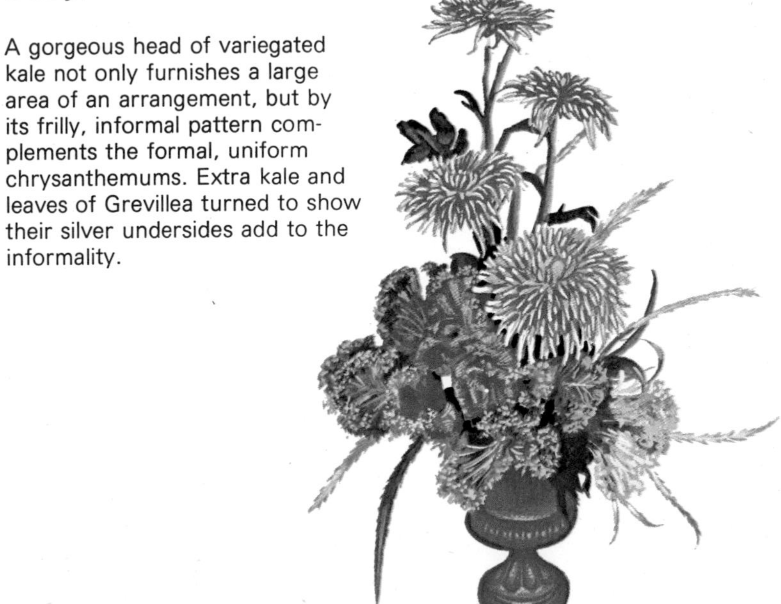

A gorgeous head of variegated kale not only furnishes a large area of an arrangement, but by its frilly, informal pattern complements the formal, uniform chrysanthemums. Extra kale and leaves of Grevillea turned to show their silver undersides add to the informality.

Containers and colors can be selected to suit the room in which the flower arrangement stands. In this arrangement for the kitchen, a copper saucepan holds everlasting flowers.

As I said earlier, if flowers are to be an important part of your interior decoration they should be neither chosen nor displayed too casually. With a little thought you can get them working for you.

You can use your flowers to create illusions. If your rooms are low, try using the flower arrangements to suggest height by placing them nearer the floor than the ceiling and choose styles in which there are good vertical lines. If the opposite is true and the ceilings are high, place your flowers on shelves, tall, slim tables, or torchères, or hang them in wall vases. If you have dark corners, light them up with floral pillars or cones of white, yellow or pastel tints which will reflect even the smallest amount of light. If you have patterned wallpaper use a monochrome color scheme.

You can save time and trouble if you place an arrangement where it is unlikely to be disturbed. A good place is the wall between two windows where the sun does not glare and yet it is in good light. If this wall is opposite the door they will speak a welcome.

In winter, dark browns of preserved materials give a surprisingly warm impression. In summer, lots of cool greens and white give a cool, airy effect which is pleasant and restful. Your fireplace can be made to glow with flowers. A bare wall can be beautifully furnished with a wall vase.

Clever placing of certain colors will help give new proportions to the rooms. Place red flowers at the end of a room rather than in the middle, because red appears to make a room smaller. Conversely, use blue to give an impression of space. A blue arrangement against a far wall in a small room will help to make it appear larger. If the setting is right, a pair of blue arrangements will achieve an even better effect.

A Byzantine cone of single chrysanthemums makes a striking decoration for the corner of a room, especially if the floral color matches that of the furnishing.

Pairing them off

There are many places in the home where a pair of floral arrangements looks more attractive than a single decoration. A mantlepiece, sideboard, a long side tab!e, or a dressing table can be given new beauty and importance this way. For parties, a buffet table can be made both attractive and entertaining if it is decorated with pairs of arrangements.

You really do not need many more flowers for a pair of arrangements than for one large one. If the theme of two floral ornaments fits in well with your interior decor schemes you might consider making a semi-permanent framework of preserved materials which is attractive enough to stand alone yet capable of being dressed up for parties. Nicely curved branches of willow or broom, for example, terminating in a cluster of preserved leaves and a knot of some lovely dried fruits, such as camphor buds or agave seed-pods, can be quickly brought to life bx a single orchid or a little curve of a few blooms of some other kind. A tube for holding tablets pushed in among the leaves will hold water for them.

Narcissi, tulips, irises and hyacinths, in bud and bloom, and maple and viburnum, look well raised on a pair of old Sheffield plate candlesticks.

It is not wise to make first one arrangement and then the other to match. Somehow the flowers that are left never seem to pair. Instead, assemble both arrangements side by side and if one has a low stem which flows to the right, try to find a similar stem which flows to the left in the other.

Obviously, it will depend upon where you stand the pair what their style should be. You might want them to be quite formal and symmetrical. On the other hand, they might look much more attractive and effective if they were asymmetrical. Supposing, for example, you placed a pair on the mantelpiece, one on each side of a picture. You could shape each into a crescent so that the picture would be 'embraced' within the curve made by each of them.

Alternatively, you could arrange the flowers in a tall triangle, each upright following a parallel line with the frame of the picture and its base running along below it. If you want to 'spread' the width of the shelf or the wall against which it stood, the base of the triangles could run in the other direction.

When you make a pair of arrangements, assemble them both at the same time so that you can make sure that they are equally balanced.

USING ONLY A FEW FLOWERS

It is not necessary to use a great many flowers to create a beautiful arrangement. I have made many in which only one flower was featured and I often use just three blooms—the result of dividing a market bunch of a dozen into four so that I can spread the flowers around the home.

Sometimes a scarcity of flowers inspires you to create a decoration in which the beauty of the individual flower becomes revealed. Japanese flower arrangement, an ancient art practiced for centuries, uses very few flowers or little plant material, but relies instead on stylized line, beautiful containers, and other accompaniments. This and other modern oriental styles derived from it have influenced the art of flower arrangement all over the world.

Western flower arrangement has, in the past, been robust in character—after all, in temperate climates, plant materials are plentiful. However, with the increase of population and the growth of commercial flower production, with warmer homes where the atmosphere hastens the maturity of cut flowers so that they become a costly item of expenditure, with less time to spend on doing the flowers and also with a new look at indoor decoration generally, there is now a tendency for arrangers to use fewer flowers *en masse* and to concentrate instead on the beauty of line.

Such arrangements are often exciting and sometimes even dramatic but, like all floral decorations, they need to suit

their surroundings. Usually, they look their best in a contemporary setting, but they can be made to harmonize by observing one or two points, for instance, choosing a container in character with the rest of the room.

We shall see, in the pages to come, how each line has meaning and in a well-designed arrangement if even one of them were removed, the arrangement would look incomplete.

The eye becomes trained to appreciate line. It is my experience that a new flower arranger often tends to try to mass line, arranging say, many bare twigs where three or five would have been enough. Only later does he realize that space and voids also have decorative values. You will soon find that a space left between lines accentuates their beauty.

Arrangements using the minimum of materials: (*Left*) A single hyacinth bloom and prunings from a clematis. (*Above*) Even a cabbage leaf is beautiful enough to accompany three daffodils. (*Right*) One calla lilly with a beautiful leaf and two rushes are enough for a lovely arrangement if stems are skillfully placed.

The tallest stem which represents heaven is known as *shin*, its tip should always be over its base. The second stem, *soe*, is two-thirds the height of the main stem. *Hikae*, representing man, always assumes a lowly position and again is shorter than the stem which precedes it. This rule applies when flowers are grouped together or when they stand apart, as these irises do.

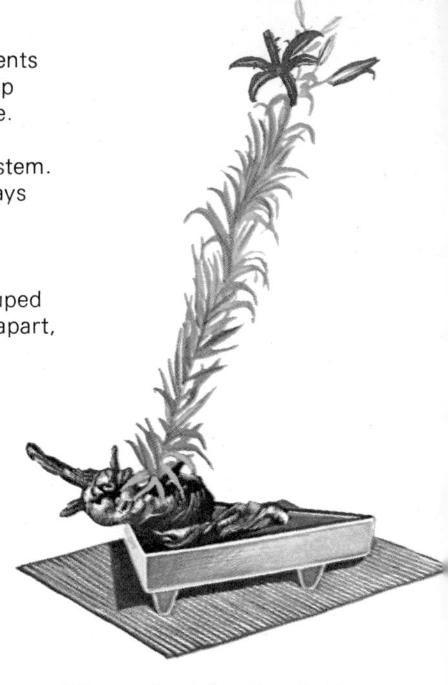

The principles behind oriental design

Rules for Japanese arrangements are strict but helpful. Those who wish to follow them faithfully will need to study hard for a long time—not only floral art but also philosophy! Others who do not wish to be too bound by rules can also benefit by studying them, for they are based on good sense.

The basic shape is an irregular triangle, the main lines of which are described by three stems, known as *shushi*. Some arrangements call for additional stems and these, known as *jushi*, should

always be placed within pattern of the *shushi*.

Centuries ago, a teacher reverently taught that these three stems represented heaven, earth and man. They are known as *shin, soe* and *hikae*. *Shin* is of the greatest importance and is always the tallest. This stem should be curved and its tip should always be over its base, a sensible rule because this always leads to good balance and pleasant placement. If the branch or stem is undulating it may move away from the center on its upward course, but it should return immediately over its base.

The *soe* is next in importance and is placed to the side of the main stem. As it rises from the surface of the water, *shin* and *soe* should run closely together but after a little space the *soe* should move away to follow its own path, reaching two-thirds the height of the main stem. *Hikae,* the short, third stem, assumes a lowly position. This should always be kept low in an arrangement and should flow forward, giving the arrangement a third dimension, although it should not be allowed to assume a drooping position. The *jushi* are added last, usually three or five are sufficient.

Picture or scenic arrangements

Today, many people are interested in Ikebana, which although it means 'keeping cut flowers alive in water', is really Japanese flower arrangement as interpreted by various schools and teachers. Now, there seem to be as many styles of Ikebana as there are of Western arrangements.

Generally, though, it represents a way of using a few flowers which can be effectively arranged by following definite rules. Its popularity is due to the fact that it can be enjoyed by anyone with or without a garden, rich or poor. It is really not so very different from a simple and free-style way of arranging flowers which many of us have practiced and enjoyed for years.

As a flower arranger who has gone her own way from the beginning, I have often been delighted to find that concepts I discovered for myself have, in fact, been expounded by those who have gone before. Take Ikebana, for example, where one rule is that the water in the container is important and represents the soil from which the plants spring.

In Ikebana, also, the stem ends at the bases—which are

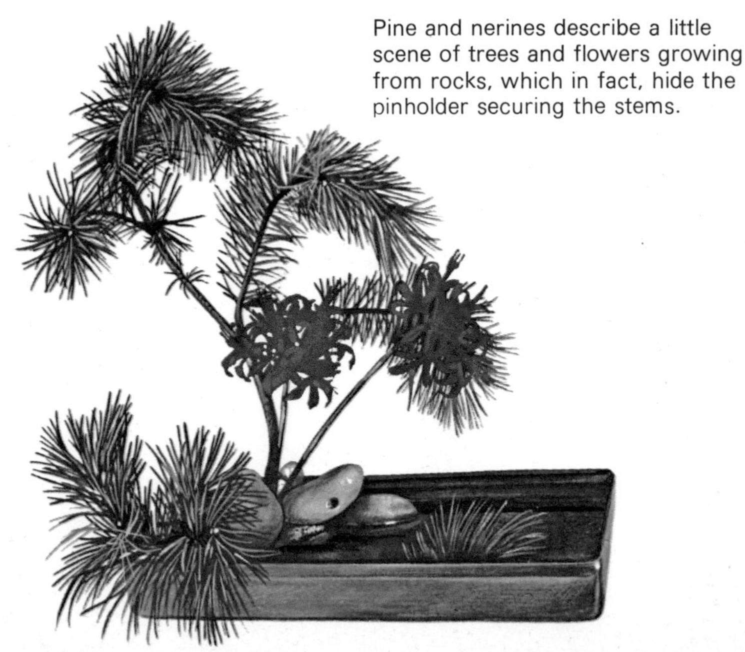

Pine and nerines describe a little scene of trees and flowers growing from rocks, which in fact, hide the pinholder securing the stems.

always visible—should be close together so that they give the illusion of combined springing up from the soil which bore them. I have always felt that the components of an arrangement, no matter what its style, should appear to spring from a common source, and this is something I have stressed in former chapters of this book.

Actually, as well as being visually pleasing, this is good sense. It is so much easier to arrange stems in a line arrangement this way just as it is so much easier to hide the mechanics of the actual arrangement when stems are close together than if they are widely distributed.

One way that this natural effect can be featured—even exploited—is when we use a few flowers and accessories in an arrangement which tells a story or describes a scene, really, an adaptation of more subtle Japanese arrangements. For these you will need firm, solid containers that suggest the earth. They should be wide enough to show an expanse of water or, alternatively, for you to spread 'grass'. They should be deep enough to sustain a good branch as well as frail flowers, if these are used.

Pussy willow, daffodils and hellebores paint a picture of spring. The Iceland-moss keeps the flowers fresh and hides their holders.

Variegated dogwood, parrot tulips and wild callas are arranged to make a crescent of color in a slim, black vase of modern design.

In this unusual arrangement, brass bowl and leaves of my own design give importance to a bunch of violets and join them in complementary harmony.

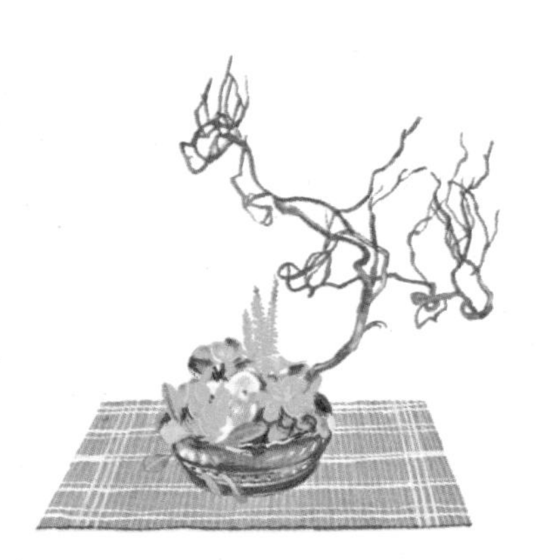

A long-lasting winter arrangement of London pride and ferns in a brass bowl. Burned gorse gives additional height, as well as providing interest.

Three English iris are arranged in a triangle. Two hosta leaves accentuate the flowing line of the flowers and lotus seed heads provide an attractive contrast of texture.

Two separate groups of snow-drops standing on pinholders arranged with sprays of wild ivy tell a story of spring gardens. The piece of wood provides a decorative base.

Only three chrysanthemum blooms are used, but swirled aspidistra leaves and thin cattails give them height and add interest to the arrangement.

Seven short-stemmed tulips sit in an arc of grevillea leaves. This is, in fact, two triangular arrangements linked together by one center flower.

A handful of flowers are placed in a modern Scandinavian mug. The daffodils are first tied together in the hand and later wedged in place with the bunch of primroses and ivy.

Accessories are both helpful and important

If you want to paint an attractive picture you need materials as well as inspiration, but the difference between the flower arranger and the painter is that to the flower arranger materials are often the source of inspiration.

A wise decorator builds up a good store of accessories. These are likely to be extremely varied and there is no limit to what you can use, except for competition, when the schedule will define what or what is not allowed. Today's 'pop' floral artists even go so far as to use bed springs and feathers among other things. My own tastes lead me to search for materials from the same basic sources as the flowers, although I also like to use shells and other marine objects.

If you decide to stock a store cupboard for your arranging you will find that you are never at a loss for something to place with any type of flower as it comes into season. There are a few materials which, to me at any rate, seem classic. Shells, for example, seem to suit all flowers equally well.

Obviously, as these vary so considerably, some shells will be more suitable for certain blooms or plant materials than others. However, there is something akin to flowers in the satin texture and rainbow colors of some, or to the bark of trees in the rough grainy surfaces of others.

A crescent of five yellow daffodils within the leaf-shape of a sea-fan. The curve is repeated in the scallop shells at the base of the flowers.

Candles and leaves are classic accessories for flowers. Here shadow leaves, dyed red to match the anemones, hold three matching candles in their curving line.

I have a selection which ranges from some tiny yellow periwinkles to scatter in a glass bowl holding daffodils, to great clams in which flowers and plants are arranged.

Leaves of all kinds may be pressed and preserved and set aside to be used at some other time. Some can be skeletonized and can be bought under the name of 'shadow' leaves. These are usually magnolia although often Ficus is included. You can preserve your own foliage. I describe how this is done in the section on dried flowers.

In complete contrast to such natural objects are candles which help the flower arranger in providing color, either when this is scarce or lacking altogether, or in setting the scene. If you have a stately colored candle as the center pivot in an arrangement you will need only a few flowers to accompany it.

Good companions

Driftwood is another classic accessory that shares the beauty of a composition as much with an orchid as a daisy. However, I feel that it must be true driftwood, worn smooth and silky by the action of sea and sand. Sometimes a simulated driftwood is prepared by stripping the bark from a branch, but it does not really please me.

Lichen-covered branches are also very beautiful and well

An accessory to flowers can play more than one role. Here, five parrot tulips are supported, as well as supplemented, by the driftwood, shells and rocks.

Cattails or reed mace and the true rushes may be dried and kept to use time and time again. Cones and preserved leaves suit autumnal flowers.

A towering branch of hazel catkins, which will open nicely in the warmth of a room, and a spray of ivy has transformed a low bunch of violets into a decoration suitable for the corner of a room.

worth using. Actually, if you handle them carefully and spray the lichen occasionally, they can be used many times. Sometimes you can find lichen-festooned larch branches which are also thick with cones.

Fresh, edible mushrooms can be used, especially in table and buffet decorations. If you have no young children in the house you can also use the more brightly colored toadstools. Best of all are the tree-oysters, a bracket fungi, which you see attached to tree trunks. These dry naturally, with no special treatment. I like to use clusters of this fungus among green leaves at the foot of a branch of early spring blossom.

Branches of early blossom seem a natural choice but some, catkins and pussy willow, for instance, can be dried and used for many weeks.

However, for a scenic arrangement, look for a nicely shaped living branch and let it play the part of a tree in the arrangement.

There are many grasses which can be stored successfully. Do not think of them only as accompaniments for dried flowers; some look pretty with fresh flowers, too.

Thick stems are not always easily impaled on a pinholder, but if the stem is split upward for about the same length as the depth of the water the two parts can then be easily impaled.

Sometimes, driftwood can be arranged like any other stem. Here, some of the snag ends of the wire netting stem holder in the vase have been wrapped around the lower two or three inches of the driftwood.

Some of the weight of this piece is supported by the edge of the container, but extra security is given by passing florist wire around the driftwood and passing the ends through the points of the pinholder.

Techniques for arrangement

If you are going to employ all kinds of accessories you must be able to arrange and position them with confidence. There is no virtue in doing flower arrangement the hard way. If an easy way does not appear to exist, look for it or devise one for yourself. Often what appears to be an important visual part of an arrangement or composition is also of practical use. For example, stones and shells can be used to hold down pinholders which are supporting heavy stems or used to wedge leaning branches and

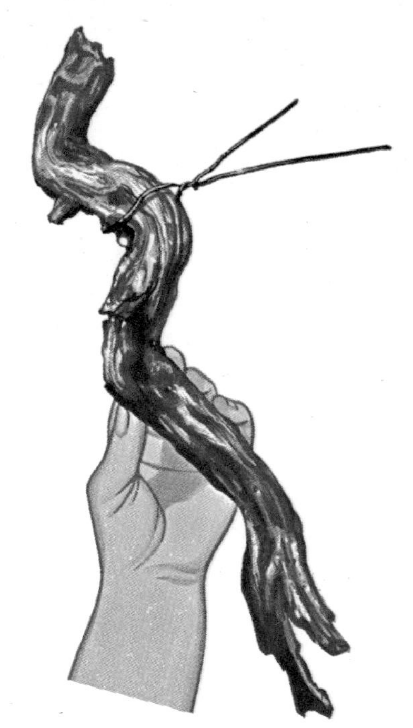

If a piece of driftwood is to flow over the rim of a container, it should be mounted on florist wire. The ends of the wire can then be easily inserted into the stem holder.

to hide other means employed to keep materials well anchored.

As long as it does not show, do not hesitate to use a wire to ensure that a stem is firmly held. I find that one 18-gauge florist wire, or two or more if a thicker gauge is needed, bent like a hairpin, is one of the best means of holding a crooked piece of driftwood in position over the rim of a container. Pass the wire over the wood and the legs down firmly into the stem holder. This is sometimes effective in holding down a branch when you want it to flow downward in a low line. Use long wires for deep vases.

Pieces of driftwood can be mounted on wires or they can be screwed onto a wooden base. Usually, you will find that it is possible to stand one piece upright and then straddle it with another. The pinholders and rocks do the rest. However, various gadgets have been invented by some flower arrangers and are sold through flower arrangement societies.

Fungi can usually be mounted by inserting an 18-gauge wire in the soft base. Cocktail sticks may also be used.

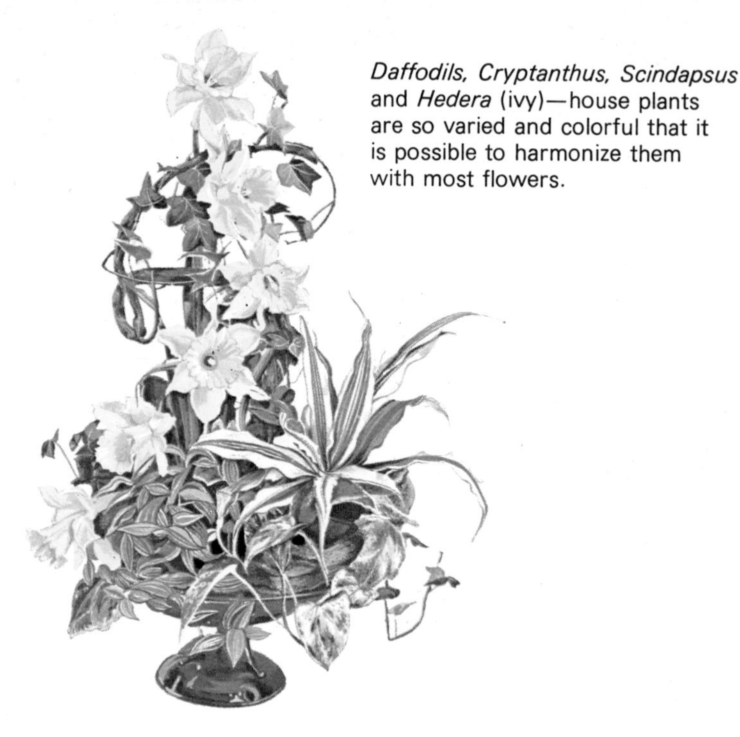

Daffodils, Cryptanthus, Scindapsus and *Hedera* (ivy)—house plants are so varied and colorful that it is possible to harmonize them with most flowers.

LONG-LASTING ARRANGEMENTS

Among the many accessories for flower arrangement we ought to consider the most natural of all—entire plants. Often, you can arrange a plant with a root as a focal point, a rosette of London pride, a soft, silver-gray verbascum, or a gloriously colored ornamental cabbage, for example. You can also arrange cut flowers and pot plants together in a *pot-et-fleur* arrangement and in this way devise ways and means of making long-lasting arrangements.

It is also possible to make the ensemble in such a way that the flowers are easily removed and replaced after they have faded as some plants will go on for months even though they may be tilted or raised to suit the arrangement.

If you like *pot-et-fleur,* which offers a form of flower arrangement as well as of indoor gardening, you will find that the accessories referred to in the previous section are essential. You will want plenty of material to hide, wedge and support pots.

Long-lasting *Cymbidium* orchids, *Dracaena, Cordyline and Cryptanthus,* their pots hidden by driftwood are arranged with yucca seed pods in a pedestal vase.

If you are also a greenhouse.gardner you will be able to create a great variety of *pot-et-fleur* arrangements, for you will have the facilities to look after and revive faded pot plants until they are once again lovely enough to accompany flowers. You could also propagate a selection of plants with *pot-et-fleur* arrangements in mind.

Plant and flower arrangements can be designed to fit in with your color schemes just as arrangements of flowers alone. You will find also that they can be just as dramatic in appearance and as exciting as outline. It all depends on what kind of plants you choose.

Many of us have containers which are really too large to be filled with flowers, yet these look lovely filled with plants and colored with fresh-cut blooms. You will find also that *pot-et-fleur* can be as elegant as a flower arrangement, especially when it is displayed in a pedestal vase. Keep this in mind when you are selecting plants. Choose some which will scramble prettily over the rim, others that will tower above them and some that can be tilted.

How the containers are filled

It is best to arrange the pot plants and the vessels to hold water for the flowers at the same time so that one can wedge, hold and hide the other. In most containers you can use Florapak or Oasis into which either the whole pot or just its base (according to the depth of the container) can be pushed. You will also find that plants can be easily and firmly tilted this way. Another advantage in using Florapak or Oasis is that when dampened the evaporation creates a micro-climate around the plants which is beneficial to them.

The containers for the flowers themselves will have to suit the size of the arrangement as well as the thickness of the flowers' stems, although if you have used Florapak or Oasis you can also arrange the flower stems in this.

I have several metal cones, painted green so that they are inconspicuous, of various sizes and lengths. I also have some mounted on thin canes. Other vessels I use are individual cigar tubes, tablet bottles, cream cartons, plastic funnels and metal florist cones. The latter just hold a cylinder of Oasis and are useful for strong-stemmed flowers. Party balloons filled with water and tied to a flower stem will make a creeper 'bloom'. Mounted containers enable you to arrange flowers at different levels.

Wide-mouthed containers, such as the cream cartons, need stem holders in them. I find, too, that it often helps to put a small screw of netting in the mouth of a cone, otherwise all the stems drop in vertically.

You can also use soil, sand, bulb fiber or peat as a 'plunge' or as packing for the pot plants. Not only does a covered surface look more attractive but it slows down evaporation. Mosses look attractive, bun mosses especially so. Iceland moss or lichen needs to be pushed in firmly so that it stands well. Watch that they do not siphon the water out.

(*Top*) Vessels to hold water for the flowers can be pushed down among the plants and hidden by them. (*Center*) Plants need to be selected for their practical value as well as for their beauty. Widespread plants, like this chlorophytum, furnish the center of the arrangement and conceal the vessel for the flowers plunged behind it. (*Bottom*) *Pot-et-fleur* arrangements can be simple like this container holding a syngonium and a holly ivy.

Flowers which suit pot plants

Some flowers seem to have a natural affinity with greenhouse-grown pot plants, and you can feel this even if you have no botanical knowledge. Generally speaking, those which have very leafy or very downy or hairy stems look ill at ease and often unattractive. Where the pot plants themselves have a lot of leaves, flowers with other foliage is distracting. An exception to this rule is the rose, which seems to fit in with everything else, but even here it might be necessary to remove a few leaves. Save them to arrange low in the container and use them to wedge the stems in place and to hide the rim.

Callas look well—but then many of the house plants are aroids, which probably accounts for it. Smooth-stemmed bulb flowers are ideal. In fact a *pot-et-fleur* offers one a way to use just three blooms from a divided bunch which I described in a former chapter.

It is not always the upper surface of a leaf which is the most vivid. Look below and there you will often find the most gorgeous hues. Match white and creamy tints with

Arranged in a large, dried fungus, *Dracaena sanderiana* flanks the driftwood, *Cordyline terminalis* spreads between the tulips, *Cryptanthus tricolor* nestles below.

chlorophytum, iby, *Cryptanthus tricolor, Dracaena sanderiana* and *Scindapsus aureus.*

Many plants carry somewhere on them, perhaps on stems, stipules or bracts, that lovely glowing plant purple—nearer to magenta than violet. Many pink flowers are really a tint of this color. Place them together and you will see. Try *Cordyline terminalis* with double pink tulips.

Study a few plants and you will find the lavender blue of Dutch iris, the rosy red of nerines, all the subtle tints and tones—and the greens—of orchids, the soft hues of modern lilies and the gay tulip colors. And even if you have no great collection and must rely only on the old and well-tried favorites, such as ivy or aspidistra, you will find the strong greens offer fine foil for all floral colors. Shells, dried seed heads and fresh fruits can be mixed in a *pot-et-fleur* to add color and will look delightful.

Another pleasant thing is that many of the house plants have foliage which bears some resemblance to the leaves of the flowers. As so many of these flowers are marketed without their own foliage, the plants fill a need.

Smooth-stemmed flowers, such as callas (really zantedeschias) and bulbous iris, look well with *Sansevieria, Cyperus, Scindapsus, Tradescantia* and ivy.

DRIED FLOWERS

At the beginning of this book I said that if you want your flowers to live for many days, you must see that they are young and in perfect condition when you pick or buy them. This is so, but under certain conditions no flowers can live for long. Central heating, for example, can kill frail flowers very quickly. The *pot-et-fleur* arrangements described in the previous chapter are better for such conditions than cut flowers alone because a growing plant raised in a greenhouse and later supplied with humidity will go on growing. But even plants succumb eventually.

Fortunately, there are many flowers, leaves and other plant materials which will stand up to the hottest and driest atmospheres. These are the everlastings, immortelles and all the fascinating perpetuelles. With these you need never be without flower arrangements. Do not imagine for one minute that they are dull. They can be as bright or, alternatively, as subtly colored as you wish.

I have many of these dried-flower arrangements myself. In fact, they are not reserved for winter decoration only but tend to become permanent decorations. There is such a wide range of materials that it is possible to select dainty, summery, feminine flowers such as soft pink daisies, roses or blue hydrangeas for bedrooms or other places where pastel tints are best and more robust colors and textures for hall or living rooms.

Blue echinops or globe thistle, with white statice and lavender in a Chinese bowl with matching colors make a charming and long-lasting table decoration.

Mostly from my garden—pressed vine leaves, achillea, strawdaisies, golden rod, tulip and plantain seed heads, barley and wild rushes.

Surprising as it may sound, you can wash some of these everlastings. Then they can be dried out and rearranged.

Many of the perpetuelles can be used to complement and supplement arrangements of fresh flowers, and I have referred to them from time to time in previous chapters. For this reason, it is wise to collect more than you anticipate using for dried decorations alone.

From varied helichrysums you can make many color schemes. With these are achillea, orange seed pods of *Iris foetidissima,* clematis seed heads and burdock.

The everlastings

As you know, most flowers will, when cut and left out of water, just shrivel and die, but there are some which produce blooms with tough, papery or straw-like petals which remain stiff and firm. If these are gathered at the correct time, before they are pollinated and begin to make seed, they will keep their shape, form and color.

Most of these plants are from the daisy or *Compositae* family. These are the everlastings and immortelles. There are both annual and perennial kinds. There are some lovely varieties and strains of these, particularly helichrysums. The annual form of this comes in white, yellow, gold, orange, pale pink, rose, red, crimson and deep bronze, which is almost black.

True everlastings can be distinguished by the papery or straw-like texture of the flower parts. But there are other flowers which, although they are not 'straw flowers' can, in fact, be dried quite naturally. These are the perpetuelles. When dried, they do not retain their beauty quite so well as the true everlastings. Even so, they are useful and decorative. Some unexpectedly fresh-looking flowers come into this category. Larkspurs and delphiniums, for example, as well as golden rod, hydrangeas, some roses and pompon chrysanthemums look very pretty in dried arrangements.

Ornamental grasses to go in winter bouquets have been cultivated for centuries. The great quaking grass, *Briza maxima;* Job's tears, *Coix Lacryma Jobi;* squirrel's tail, *Hordeum jubatum* and hare's tail, *Lagurus ovatus* are favorites.

There are also wild grasses well worth gathering. Highly decorative are the farm cereals, oats, wheat, barley, corn (including some attractive garden hybrids) and, if you live where they are grown, rice and millet.

The important thing about all of these is that they must really be cut when the flower or grass is at the correct point of maturity; success depends on this. Young flowers' colors are clearer; their stems, stronger.

Helipterum daisies have clear yellow centers. White and yellow statice, and *Briza maxima,* the quaking grasses, surround them.

Flowers to grow

If you would like to grow some of these flowers for yourself you will find them listed in all good seedsman's catalogues. Usually available are *Ammobium alatum,* or sand flower; *Gomphrena globosa,* or Globe Amaranth; *Helichrysum bracteatum,* the straw daisy of which there are many varieties and strains; *Helipterum manglesii,* sometimes listed as *Rhodanthe manglesii* and *H. roseum,* often called *Acroclinium roseum; Limonium bonduelli, sinuatum, suworowii; limoniums* are also listed as *statice; Lonas inodora; Xeranthemum annuum, X. a. ligulosum* and *X. a. perligulosum.* There are also perennials, *Anaphalis margaritacea,* or pearly everlasting, many helichrysums, including some with attractive downy, or 'silver' foliage; and *Limonium latifolium* and *incanum.*

Among the non-everlastings are *Amaranthus caudatus,* or loves-lies-bleeding and its near relatives the showy cock's combs, or Celosia; Didiscus, the lace flower; salvias—those

showy bedding plants which are now in other colors than scarlet; *Tagetes* among which are the African and French marigolds and zinnias—but not the red ones. All of these are annuals.

There are many perennials and, before I list them, I would like to urge you to experiment with drying others. A great deal seems to depend upon the season. In hot dry summers I have found flowers like rambler roses, *Pelargoniums, Helianthemums,* cornflowers, even *Aquilegia,* dry well.

Perennials which I dry often are: many of the achilleas including the filipendulina varieties and the white ptarmica; *Echinops,* or globe thistle, and the *Eryngium,* or sea holly (the wild seashore holly will also dry but it is very prickly); gypsophila—the double is better, *Salvia farinacea,* the lovely blue salvia, stachys and verbascum. Among shrubs I dry buddleia, erica or heathers, hydrangea, lavender and catkins of all kinds.

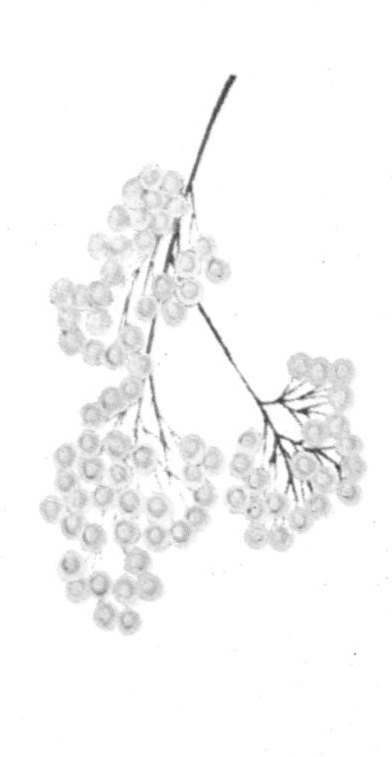

(*Left*) Seed heads, such as teasels, grasses, bulrushes, and everlastings, like helichrysums and statice, have long lives. (*Right*) Not true everlastings, but hydrangeas, larkspur and mimosa may also dry.

(*Top left*) Poppy heads are often imported, but any of the garden poppies can also be used. Green pods retain much of their color.

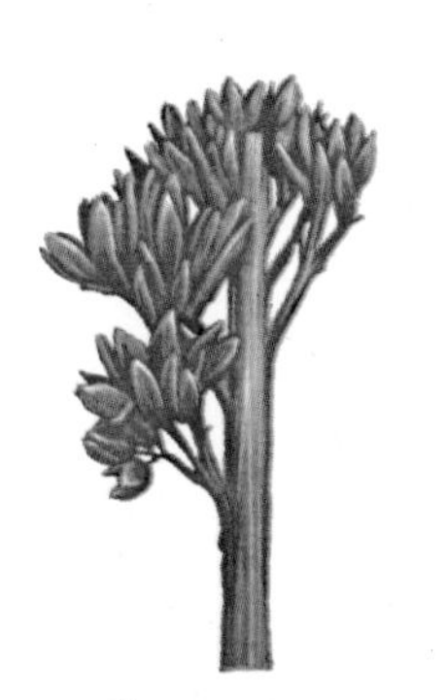

(*Middle left*) Yucca seed pods are almost wooden—a texture they share with other seed vessels of the same lily tribe. Large clusters can be divided.

(*Below left*) Sweet corn husks can be opened to make a giant 'flower'. Some of the Indian, or squaw corn, with brightly multicolored kernels looks attractive displayed this way.

(*Below*) Okra pods, the seed cases of a succulent vegetable, can be mounted individually.

(*Right*) Artichokes and cardoons are handsome perpetuelles and ideal for large arrangements. Cut them while still young.

(*Middle right*) Many trees have fruits which are well worth harvesting. Maple keys should be cut while young and brightly colored. They dry to a biscuit tint.

(*Below right*) The star thistle, and others are highly decorative, but require careful handling.

(*Below*) The gorgeous magnolia blossoms are followed by seed pods of interesting form and texture. False stems have to be attached when these are used in tall decorations.

Pressed ferns mixed with teasels, seed heads and larch cones are used as a permanent background for a few scarlet anemones arranged separately in water.

Preserving other perpetuelles

As you can see by the illustrations on the previous page, there are other parts of plants included in the ever-growing list of perpetuelles which can be dried. These are not only leaves but even roots. Seed stems of all kinds abound. Most of these dry on the plant and must be gathered before they become deteriorated by rain or frost.

Most of the true everlastings and the other flowers I have already described should be made into small bunches and hung head downward in a cool, but very dry, place. It should also be dark, for then the colors will be brightest. Sunshine and bright light will make grasses hay-like.

Always gather all materials on dry days only and before frosts occur. Remember that materials gathered in wet seasons when growth is lush take longer to dry and for this reason you should make the bunches quite small. Hang them well apart so that the air can circulate around them.

Flowers such as roses, and indeed all but the true everlastings which would become too brittle if treated this way, are often best dried quickly in a warm place, such as an airing cupboard. A rack or 'table' of wire netting will enable you to support round, flat flowers, such as zinnias and helichrysums. Insert the stem through the mesh, and let the flower rest on it.

Helichrysums sometimes sever easily from their stems. To avoid this gather the flower with a small portion of stem, insert a florist wire up the stem until the flower's center is reached, but do not let the wire penetrate it, and either hang them head downward or support them through wire mesh until the flower is dry (when stem has shriveled).

To preserve branches, feathery seed heads such as *Clematis vitalba* or old man's beard, immature seed heads or downy flower spikes such as *Verbascum,* among many other things, make a solution of one-third glycerine and two-thirds water. Mix and boil this and pour into a deep narrow vessel so that the stem ends can be stood in about two or three inches of the hot solution, according to their own length. If a tin or glass jar is used, stand this inside a bucket to prevent it from tipping over.

To skeletonize leaves let them soak for a few weeks in rain water until you can remove the outer tissues by slipping a leaf between the fingers. Then wash under running water, soak in a solution of household bleach and water. Dry in newspaper. Press flat ferns between newspaper or books under a weight until they are dry.

Drying flowers in a desiccant

You may have heard of flowers being dried by being buried in sand and this is possible but it is not really to be recommended because the sand is so heavy that it cannot be safely used to any great depth or it will damage the flower. But it is cheap! Much lighter in weight are borax and silica gel but these are more costly. However, the crystals can be used again and again. Some people mix borax and sand together. I prefer to use silica gel.

Unless you are going to have great quantities of the desiccant, enough to fill deep boxes to take the entire flower stem, the stems have to be shortened and this, in turn, means that false wire stems have to be applied later. It may also be necessary to tape them with florist tape or crepe paper tapes so that they look as natural as possible.

Airtight boxes should be used and if there is any doubt that their lids do not fit tightly these should also be sealed with tape.

The procedure is first to pour a layer of the desiccant on

Flowers may be dried by burying them in a desiccant such as silica gel, which should surround the flowers and be sifted between the petals.

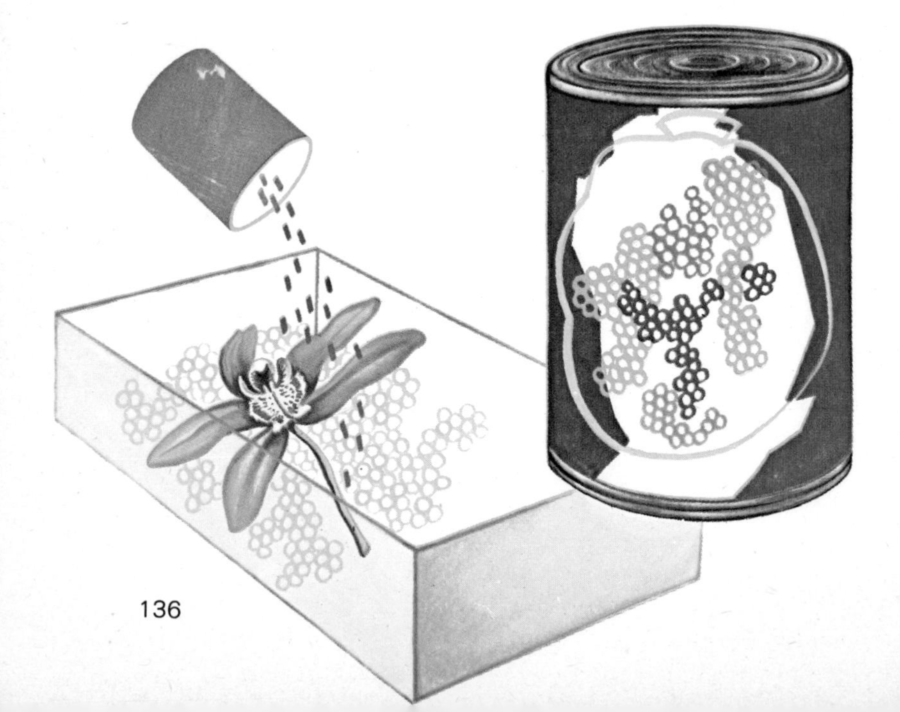

the floor of the box. Place the flowers in position on this layer according to the type of flower (e.g., whether it has a face like a pansy and will lie flat, or whether it is like a rose and will need desiccant sifted carefully in between its petals or whether it is like a flat daisy, which should be laid face down).

You will find that the upward-facing ones will have to be supported while you pour the desiccant over, under and around them so that it can flow in every crevice, for flowers must be buried. The actual time taken for a flower to dry will depend very much on the type of flower. As a general rule, flowers take from one to five days. Some kinds will dry in an airing cupboard, cornflowers and large individual florets of delphiniums, for example, and these will dry quicker than a fleshy flower. This, however, is very much a matter of trial and error. If you find that some flowers shatter when they have dried, try fixing the petals by painting the bases with gum arabic before burying. Test by gently brushing or pouring away the desiccant until a flower is exposed and can be felt.

Flat flowers, such as all the daisy family, are best placed in the desiccant head downward, but take care that they are completely covered.

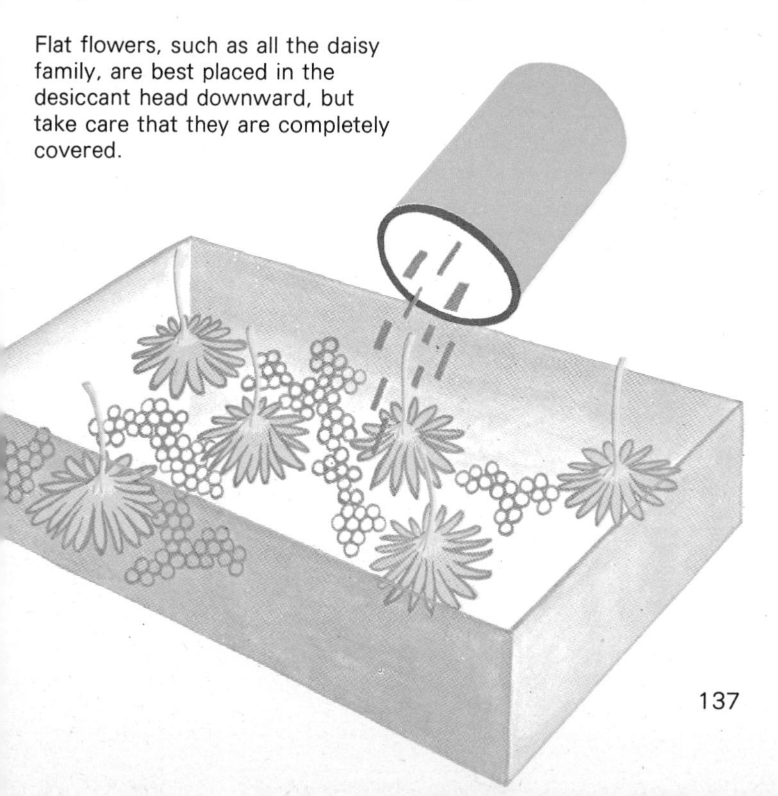

Pine cones and many other stemless scaly or rough-textured subjects can be mounted as shown. Use a long florist wire to do so, placing it between the scales. Put pressure on it so that the wire is hidden in the bases of the scales.

Twist one wire around the other and bring the two legs down to roughly the same point as one would expect the stem to be. The wire portion can be used as a stem. It can also be made longer and joined to another wire or a slim cane. Several canes can be bunched together by binding their mount wires.

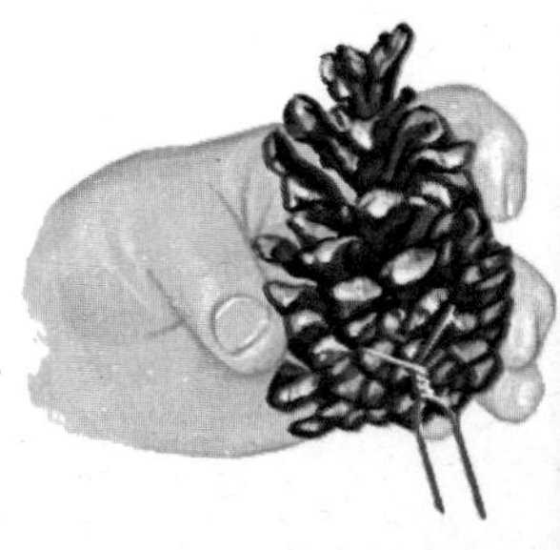

Pull the florist wire around the cone so that it fits snugly in the crevices between the scales and is hidden by them. It is possible to keep the wire quite flat against the cone's surface as the legs are brought down and under before being twisted together.

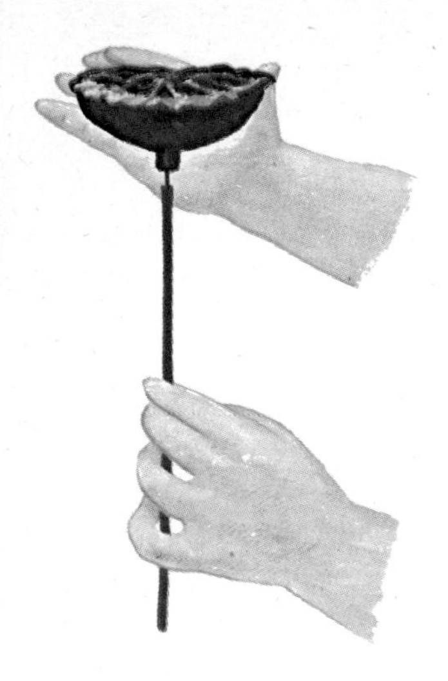

If the short stem below a subject like this lotus seed head, is soft or hollow, take a short wire and insert it up the stem as far as possible. Then push the protruding portion into the center of a hollow stem or straw. Push the ends of stem and straw together.

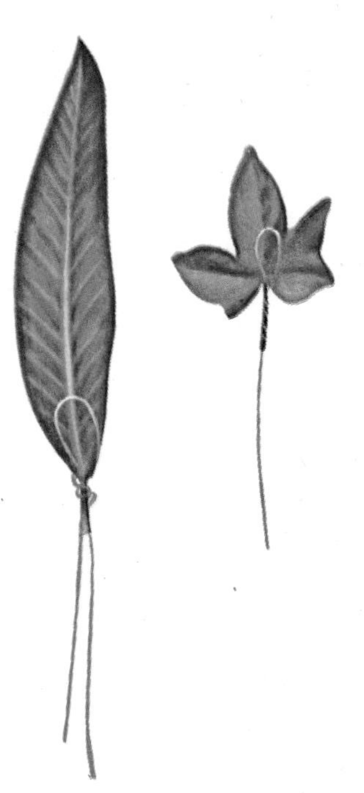

False stems of wire are usually strong enough for all but very large leaves. Mount as directed for leaf loops, below.

Smaller leaves can be slightly reinforced if the loop is laid on the back surface to reach about two-thirds the length of the leaf before the wire is passed around the stem.

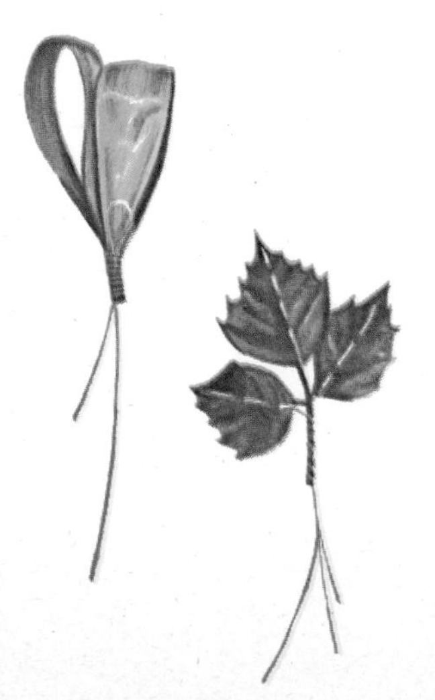

Mount leaf loops by looping one end of wire to lie against the back of the leaf. Pass the long end around the leaf or leaves binding them together. Bring it down to make the 'stem'.

Soft leaves may need to be stitched with fine wire. Do this before pressing or drying but after preserving.

Posies of field daisies, each with its own collar of ivy leaves, are simply placed in a ring around a candle in a shallow dish.

PARTY FLOWERS

Flower arrangements for parties can look lovely, but they can also be quite simple to make, their assembly taking no more than a matter of minutes.

If they are expendable, one of the prettiest ways to decorate a table is merely to place a posy or a corsage by each place. Ivy trails and other graceful foliage can help you here, for with them you can outline shapes, say a long lazy 'S' on a table surface, or festoons on a buffet table apron, and stud this foliage with neat posies at suitable intervals. My illustration of a very simple decoration made from posied daisies can be used for other kinds of flowers, and there are many variations on this theme. You can, for example, stack up bowls and make posy pyramids.

To save time you can mix your fruit and flowers on the table. Camellias, callas, chincherinchees, gladioli and orchids are just a few which can be arranged out of water so that there will be no need to worry about spillage.

Gladiolus and laurel leaves are arranged on a pinholder in a shallow vase at the back of the tray on which the fruit is arranged.

If you use cylinders or sections of dry Oasis you can stand the fruit at varying levels. Even the roundest apple will stay in place if it is lightly pressed into the plastic. At the same time these will serve to hold the flowers' stems in position.

The spicate shape of gladioli contrasts attractively with the rounded forms of most fruits. Color harmonizes easily, for in the reds, oranges, apricots and yellows of the flowers you are certain to find some of the fruit color.

So little water is needed for these flowers when they are to last for a few days that you can choose a really shallow container to hold the heavy pinholder on which they should be impaled. Being shallow, this is easily hidden. Indeed, if you can lay a tough leaf, such as laurel, over it you will be able to arrange the fruit quite close to the flowers' stems. Gladioli, daffodils and iris can be quickly arranged, for all you need to do is to bunch them with their heads at different levels, cut the stem ends level and merely press the bunch on the pinholder.

Your flowers can break the ice!

Novel flower decorations can provide a point of discussion at any party, but they should be attractive as well as original. Often originality springs from seeking a quick and easy way of displaying flowers or of creating a mass of color. Have nearby a few party accessories; cake boards on which fruit and flowers can be arranged; doilies to act as stemholders, as well as mats; heavy but low candleholders which can be hidden among flowers; and fruit spread out on the table.

In previous chapters we have seen how a flower container can be built up by using a combination of various vessels and ornaments. For a dinner party, pieces of table china matching that on which the food is being served, can be used for the flowers.

On page 54 there is an illustration showing small dishes piled one on the other. Spare lids of vegetable dishes can be used in much the same way. If they are upturned they will usually fit quite securely into a glass, sometimes even into an egg cup; it really depends on what you have available.

Pineapple candleholders sit easily in wine glasses. The doilies give each a party frill. Pompon chrysanthemum stems are threaded through the 'lace'.

A plate standing on end in a block of Oasis can hide the base of the stems of the flowers arranged behind it, while other, shorter flowers can be arranged to appear to flow out from it, thus hiding its support.

I see no reason why plant materials should not be dressed up for certain occasions. *Cycas* leaves, for example, when raised on strong false stems, make distinctive backgrounds in large arrangements. But the deep green of preserved fronds is often too heavy for the color scheme of, say, a wedding reception buffet decoration. However, if they are first lightly sprayed with clear varnish and then dusted with glitter, a transformation takes place. Silver, gold, blue, ruby and even green glitter can be used effectively on pressed or preserved ferns. Christmas tree decorations also bring a little sparkle to party arrangements. Small samples can be bought already mounted on chenille stems. Others can be mounted on pipe cleaners. They can be distributed or grouped according to the type of arrangement. Purple and green baubles look splendid arranged like bunches of grapes.

(*Left*) Tall or raised decorations suit buffet tables. Cones, like this one, enable you to use snippets of green and short-stemmed flowers. Ornaments add a party note and are mounted on pipe cleaners.

(*Right*) For special occasions, plant materials can be given a party dress of paint and glitter. Christmas tree decorations look well among flowers. They have to be mounted on false stems.

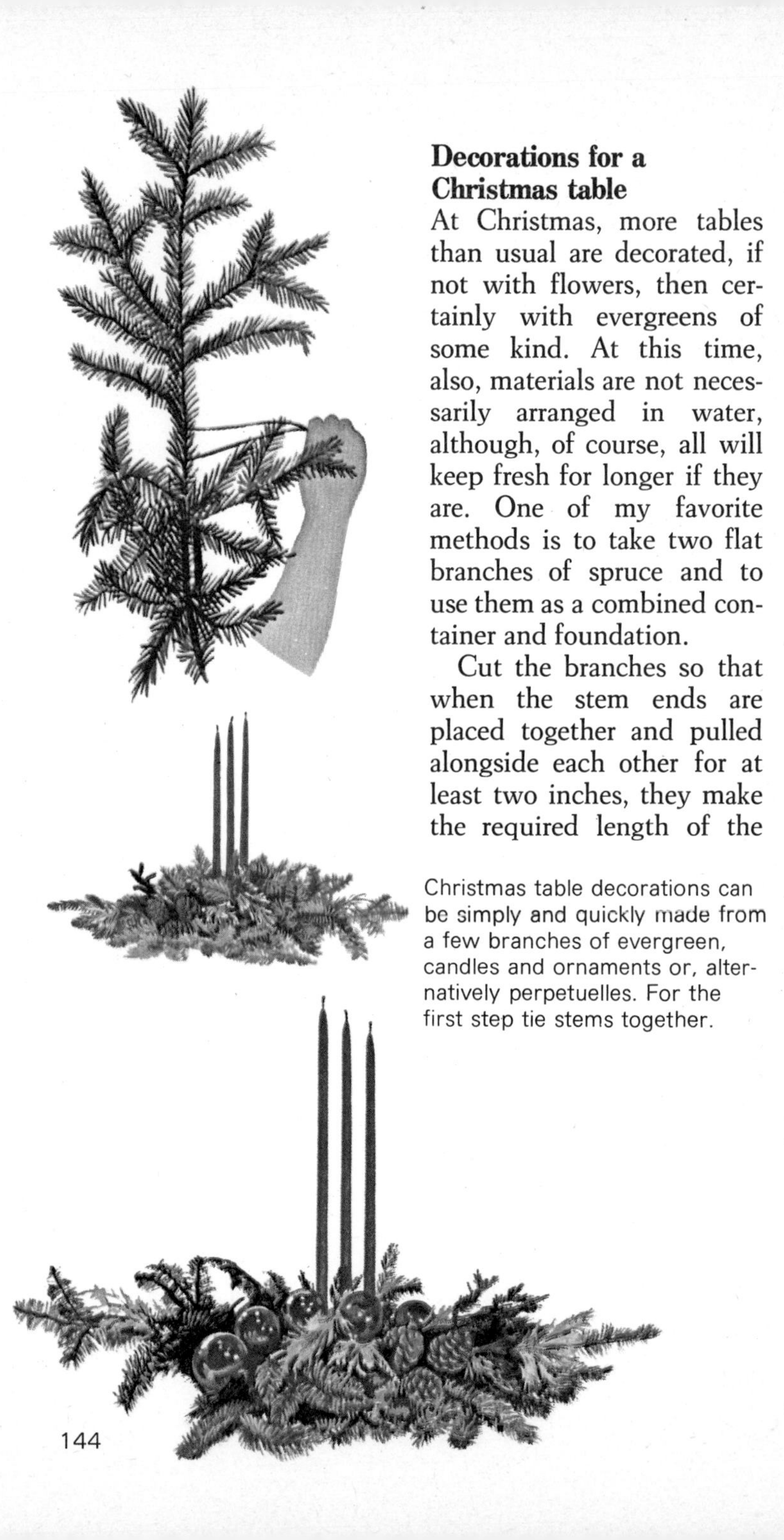

Decorations for a Christmas table

At Christmas, more tables than usual are decorated, if not with flowers, then certainly with evergreens of some kind. At this time, also, materials are not necessarily arranged in water, although, of course, all will keep fresh for longer if they are. One of my favorite methods is to take two flat branches of spruce and to use them as a combined container and foundation.

Cut the branches so that when the stem ends are placed together and pulled alongside each other for at least two inches, they make the required length of the

Christmas table decorations can be simply and quickly made from a few branches of evergreen, candles and ornaments or, alternatively perpetuelles. For the first step tie stems together.

table decoration. Secure the large stem ends firmly together. Test that the tied branches lie flat on the table.

Take a roll of wire netting, place it in the center of the decoration over the tied stems and tie it to them by threading wire or twine through the netting and around the stems. Arrange the candles pushing their bases down through the netting. Do not worry if they lean a little because they can be wedged upright as the other snippets of green are inserted in the wire around them. This is the basic shape, the 'all-round' arrangement in another guise. Use pieces of netting and single candles for small decorations.

The foliage should be varied so that you have plenty of contrast to the green. Variegated and silver downy sprigs look good, so do berries and other fruits, ornaments, everlasting lichen and even artificial toadstools!

If you prefer to make a decoration on a base, the method is rather similar. I find that cake boards are useful as foundations. Make a slight depression in the center to anchor the candle after it has passed through the wire netting. Remember the taller and heavier the candle the more netting you will need.

In this Christmas decoration, a cake board is used as a base. Wire netting holds all the foliage and the colorful ornaments contrast with the green of the plant material.

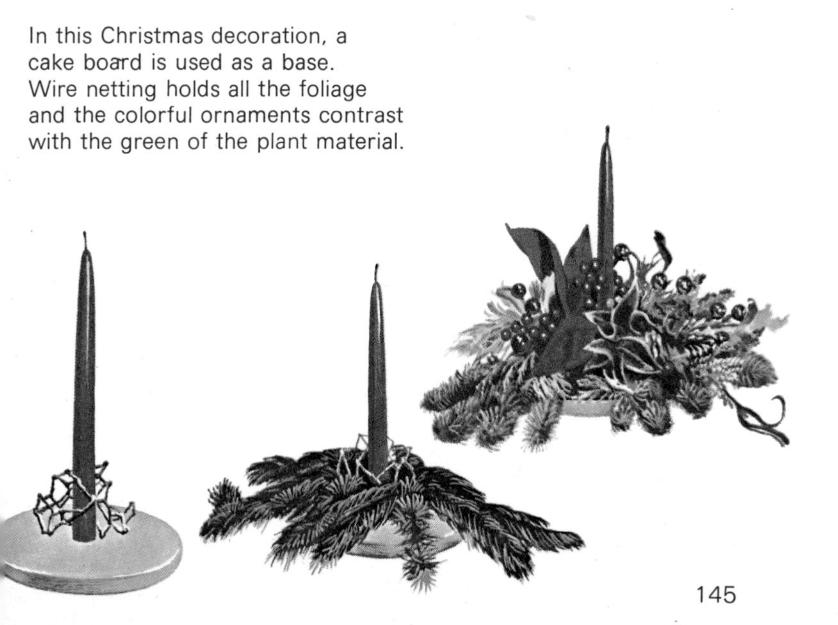

Anemones, golden cupressus and holly. To make the most of their vivid color, holly sprigs may need to have some leaves removed.

Other Christmas decorations

The flat shape of the spruce and some other evergreens used at Christmas is both useful and attractive and is well worth exploiting for its seasonal effect. If you cut a side branch you will see that it is pyramidal in outline. I like to use a branch as the background of an arrangement against which just a few blooms can be displayed.

If the flowers have short stems they can be arranged effectively quite low leaving the branch to show its shape. I have often glittered branches and hung them with stars and ornaments or with dainty glittered cones.

To add a little height and variety of shape, color and atmosphere you can arrange ornaments rising above the low-placed rounded flowers. Long, bare florist wires to support the ornaments are inconspicuous against the branch. Grade the ornaments so that the smallest are at the top.

Evergreens usually need grooming. Leaves should be wiped over with warm water, and if you want them to be really glossy use a little olive oil on them after washing. Heavily berried sprigs of holly provide more color if some of the leaves are carefully snipped away with scissors. Although some berries can be sprayed with clear varnish to keep them plump, this may turn holly berries black, so test this method first. To keep the berries plump and the evergreens fresh, arrange them in water to which a little plant food has been added.

Blue spruce seldom drops its needles; instead it is more inclined to dry like other perpetuelles. Thuja, cypress and other needles will also dry but become brittle and tend to drop off if touched. All these can be held fast if sprayed with clear varnish or painted with Polycell.

A branch of flat-growing spruce or some other evergreen makes an aptly shaped background for a few flowers in a Christmas decoration. With these forced daffodils are variegated elaeagnus and holly berries.

FLOWERS FOR EXHIBITIONS

One of the delightful things that has been promoted by flower clubs everywhere is that more flowers than ever are on exhibition and can be enjoyed by the general public who are usually overwhelmed at both the beauty of the flowers and the skill of those who arranged them.

Suddenly, it seems, our churches regain their medieval glory as a band of flower arrangers move in to celebrate a festival of flowers. Glorious country houses become young again as great vases and pedestals are set against the wall or blooms flank the great staircase. The local town hall becomes transformed as club members move in with drape backgrounds, tables and a multitude of flowers.

This is only one of the good things for which flower clubs are responsible. Another is that often beautiful arrangements are just exhibited and not judged. This does not mean that the quality of the arrangements is inferior for, always, the highest standard is demanded from anyone who has been given the honor of being allowed to exhibit.

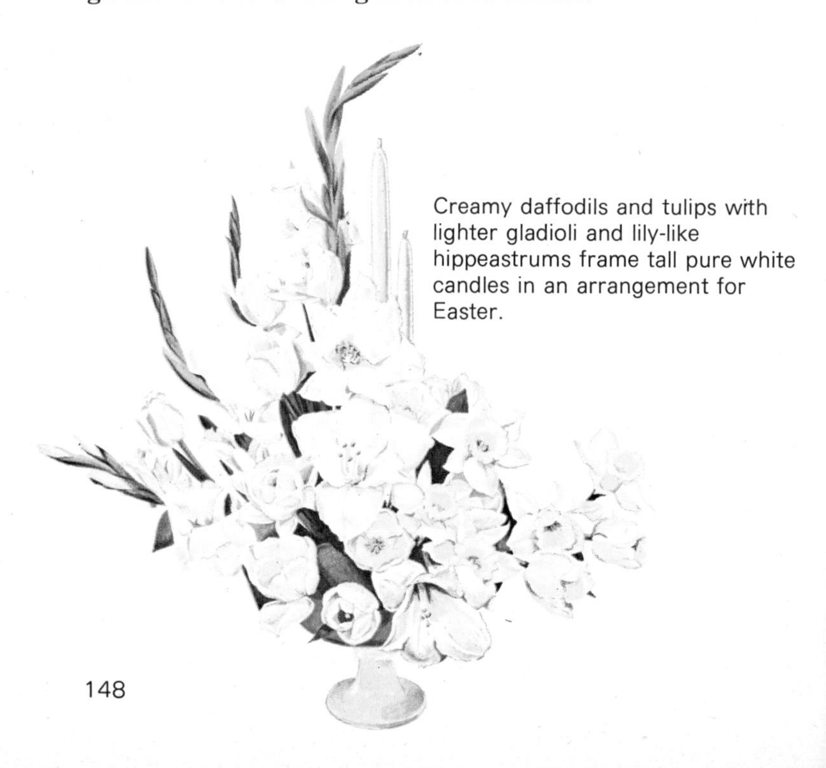

Creamy daffodils and tulips with lighter gladioli and lily-like hippeastrums frame tall pure white candles in an arrangement for Easter.

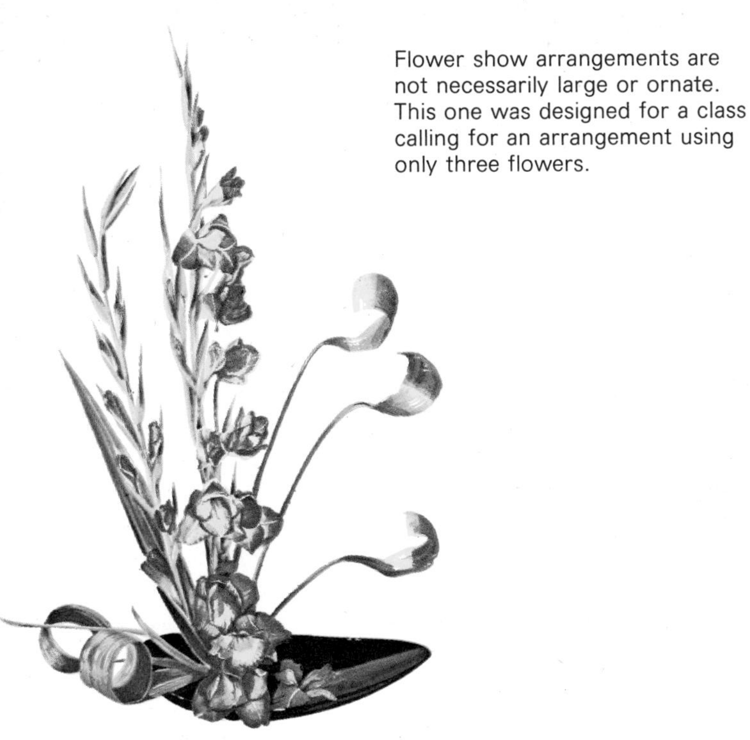

Flower show arrangements are not necessarily large or ornate. This one was designed for a class calling for an arrangement using only three flowers.

However, there are also times when competitions are held and flower arrangements are judged. These have to be assembled and staged and later, judged, according to the schedule drawn up by the club.

It is not always flower clubs alone who hold competitions, but when they do, all exhibits are judged by accredited judges strictly according to the rules laid down by the flower club. At other flower shows, usually held by a horticultural society, a judge may not be called upon to observe the same rules.

Inevitably, the schedule must be the guide. This also varies considerably according to the size and nature of the flower show. A small town's show schedule may be very simple and give the competitor little guidance, while a larger show schedule is not only likely to have many more classes but also to define much more clearly what is expected. If the arrangement is 'not according to schedule' it is likely to be disqualified and passed over when judging takes place.

Before using grasses, berries or any plant material other than flowers, check that this is according to regulations.

Attention to detail is important

As a judge, I have so often been disappointed when my co-judges and I have regretfully had to pass over a really lovely arrangement because one little thing was against the schedule rules. For example, in an arrangement which calls for foliage only, someone may use a flower bud or an immature seed head or a cone, because they are green.

There is sometimes misunderstanding over the use of a term which to the botanist may mean one thing and to the layman another. For instance, to me 'fruits' could include anything which follows a flower whether it be a gourd, a seed pod or a banana, but the schedule makers might mean edible fruit only. It is as important for those who draw up schedules to make them concise and perfectly clear so the arranger can interpret them correctly.

The size of an arrangement is also important. Because space is often at a premium, flower arrangers are given a precise place for each exhibit. A good schedule should inform you just what the dimensions are.

I find that exhibitors tend to misunderstand the importance of these dimensions. Usually those who stage the show arrange it so that each exhibitor has his or her own alcove. Often I have stood before an arrangement which was so large that it crowded its space and lost its beauty in doing so. On the other hand, I have often admired an arrangement and regretted that because it was so small and seemed swamped by its surroundings, that it could not be given a prize.

Among the qualities that judges look for in an arrangement are balance and proportion. If the arrangement is not scaled to its surroundings its own good balance and proportions will not be evident. Many arrangers find that it helps them to make a practice arrangement at home.

Many a beautiful arrangement has failed to win the top prize because one stem, leaf or flower has wilted before the judges got to it. Materials for show must be well prepared and hardened. The earliest pages in this book deal with care and transport of flowers.

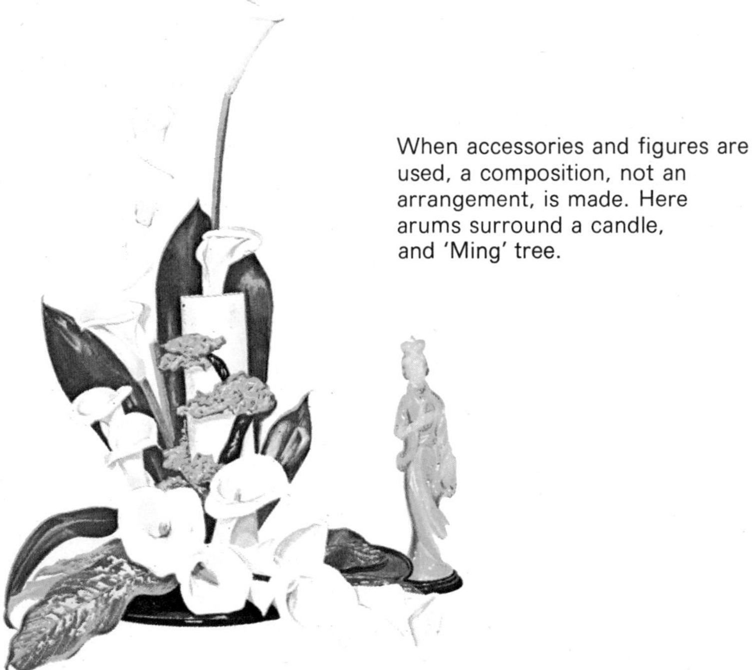

When accessories and figures are used, a composition, not an arrangement, is made. Here arums surround a candle, and 'Ming' tree.

The color and condition of materials can do much to accentuate the beauty and quality of an arrangement. Accessories used must also be in perfect condition.

Advice on staging

It often surprises me at an exhibition to see an arrangement into which, obviously, so much time and thought has gone, displayed on a piece of fabric which is creased and sometimes even soiled. Judges like to see attention paid to the slightest detail. Foliage should be groomed, vases cleaned and drapes pressed.

Spend a little time when all is done looking hard and critically for faults. In one class I once judged, what should have been the first prize had to be given less points because the tallest and most noticeable stem, a foxglove, had its top two or three inches crawling with aphides. Often a spray of lovely foliage will have holes cut in its leaves by various insects.

Make certain also that none of the materials is causing a siphon. The old Japanese rule about the lower stem not resting on the container may be based on common sense. Sometimes when a leaf, expecially a downy one, is resting on the rim, it siphons the water from the vase on to the table.

Another thing which sometimes gets overlooked is the

A well-groomed appearance is important and particularly so where the arrangement depends upon the contrasts of textures and shapes rather than on vivid colors. Echeveria, *Begonia Rex* foliage, zebrina and the immature flowers of eryngium harmonize with the pure metal sheen of the pewter stand and plate.

(*Below*) Stem holders can be hidden by all kinds of accessories. Here, the strata of the stones repeat both the line and colors of the stems of the yellow callas, really zantedeschias. The grays in them repeat shades.

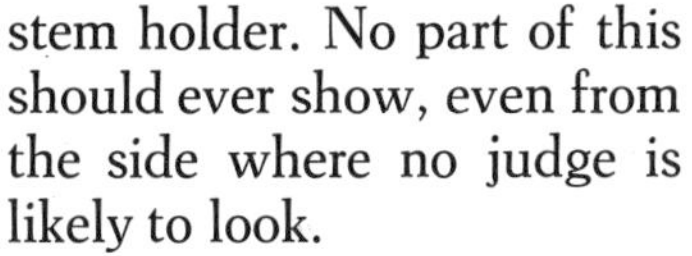

stem holder. No part of this should ever show, even from the side where no judge is likely to look.

It is my experience that stem holders are often much larger than they need to be. As long as anchorage is secure, pinholders can be quite small and, consequently, easily hidden. As I commented in an earlier chapter, the means employed to hide a stem holder can often add to the character and general effectiveness of the arrangement. Make sure that whatever accessories you employ suit the mood and style of the arrangement.

Interpretive arrangements

In many flower shows there are classes in which you are asked to interpret a subject. Sometimes the show itself has a theme, in which case the classes will be related to the overall title. At other times, just one or two classes may be included to give the exhibitor an opportunity of creating something out of the ordinary. Usually, these classes are of great interest to the visitors to a show.

Experienced flower arrangers can take them in their stride, but during the year I seem to receive many letters from puzzled readers, new to exhibition work, who ask me to explain how they can possibly make a flower arrangement which also depicts a song title or some similar theme. This is hard for me because I know that when the arrangements are being judged some points are given for originality. The theme should be the exhibitor's own idea. Therefore, I use a simple example *The Last Rose of Summer* in which one rose is used with materials suggesting the onset of autumn.

Perhaps I should say that often what might seem a novel

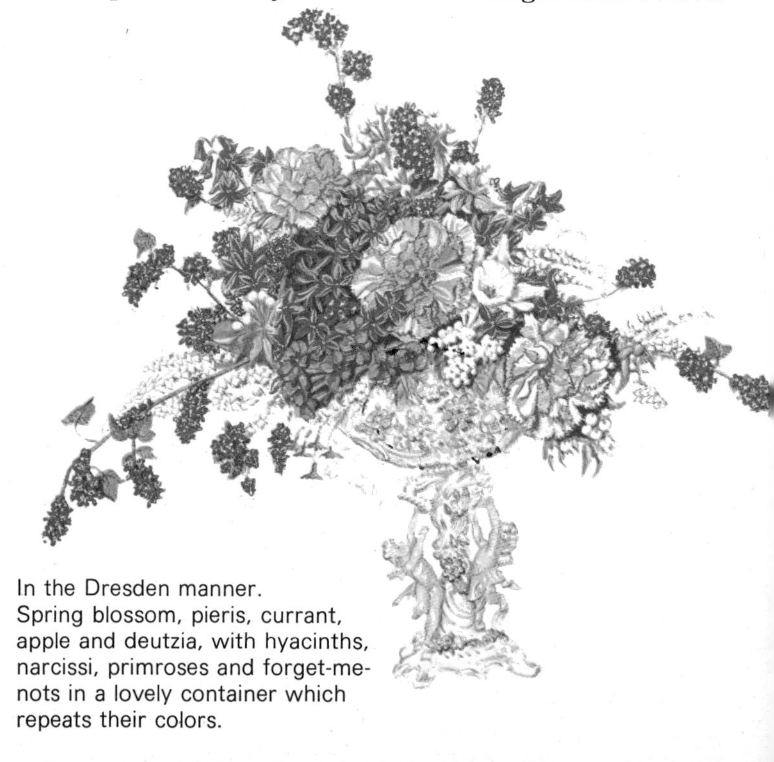

In the Dresden manner.
Spring blossom, pieris, currant, apple and deutzia, with hyacinths, narcissi, primroses and forget-me-nots in a lovely container which repeats their colors.

idea to an exhibitor may be hackneyed to a judge who visits many shows in places around the country or even around the world. Therefore originality really needs to be just that if you hope to be a prize winner.

To be given a theme is often a great deal easier than to think of one for yourself, but then you are much more likely to find another exhibitor working along the same lines as yourself. In such a situation, do not be dismayed. Continue, but remember that judging is likely to be highly competitive, so make certain that you attend meticulously to details and take care not to lose points on arrangement.

One last point. It may not have occured to you that there really are both very modern and old-fashioned flowers, distinctive enough to be recognized as such. Most of those you buy from the florist are modern introductions, so if you seek to interpret something from the past remember that you are much more likely to strike the right atmosphere if you search for flowers that were popular then.

'Heaven and Earth' was the title I gave to my little arrangement of three hydrangea blooms, ligularia leaves and clematis seed heads.

BOOKS TO READ

The Art of Flower Arrangement. Beverly Nichols. Viking, 1967.

Flower Arrangements and their Settings. George Worsnop Smith. Viking, 1967.

Flower Arrangements that Last: how to buy, dry and arrange permanent flowers. Marian Klamkin. Macmillan, 1968.

Creativity in Flower Arrangement. Frances Bode. Hearthside, 1967.

Wildflowers in Your House. Josephine von Miklos. Doubleday, 1968.

The Art of Judging and Exhibiting Flower Arrangements. Sylvia Hirsch. Crowell, 1968.

Flower Arrangement with Antiques. Beth Hemingway. Hearthside, 1965.

Flower Arrangements Anyone Can Do Anywhere. Matilda Rogers. Dodd, 1954.

Flower Arrangement in Color. Violet Stevenson. (Studio) Viking, 1961.

Decoration for the Table. Violet Stevenson. (Studio) Viking, 1965.

Flower Decorations for the Home. Violet Stevenson. Transatlantic, 1950.

Flower Decoration in European Homes. Laurence Buffet-Challié. Morrow, 1969.

1000 Beautiful House Plants and how to grow them. Jack Kramer. Morrow, 1969.

Conway's Encyclopedia of Flower Arrangement. J. Gregory. Knopf, 1957.

Conway's Treasury of Flower Arrangements. J. Gregory. Knopf, 1953.

Handbook for Flower Arrangers. Phyllis Page. International Publication Series, 1965.

INDEX

Page numbers in bold type refer to illustrations.

OTHER TITLES IN THE SERIES

The GROSSET ALL-COLOR GUIDES provide a library of authoritative information for readers of all ages. Each comprehensive text with its specially designed illustrations yields a unique insight into a particular area of man's interests and culture.

NOW AVAILABLE

PREHISTORIC ANIMALS
BIRD BEHAVIOR
WILD CATS
FOSSIL MAN
PORCELAIN
MILITARY UNIFORMS, 1686–1918
BIRDS OF PREY
FLOWER ARRANGING
MICROSCOPES & MICROSCOPIC LIFE
THE PLANT KINGDOM
ROCKETS & MISSILES
FLAGS OF THE WORLD
ATOMIC ENERGY
WEATHER & WEATHER FORECASTING
TRAINS
SAILING SHIPS & SAILING CRAFT
ELECTRONICS
MYTHS & LEGENDS OF ANCIENT GREECE
CATS, HISTORY—CARE—BREEDS
DISCOVERY OF AFRICA
HORSES & PONIES
FISHES OF THE WORLD
ASTRONOMY
SNAKES OF THE WORLD
DOGS, SELECTION—CARE—TRAINING